MW00785854

INFORMATION GAP ACTIVITIES
IN THE CONTENT AREAS

Nicholas V. Flammia

Delta Publishing Company
A Division of Delta Systems Co., Inc.
1400 Miller Parkway
McHenry, IL 60050 USA
(815) 363–3582 Toll Free (800) 323–8270
www.delta–systems.com

Copyright © 2003 Nicholas V. Flammia

All rights reserved. Permission is given for individual classroom teachers to reproduce the student activity and illustration pages for classroom use. Reproduction of these materials for an entire school system is strictly forbidden.

Printed in the United States of America

10 9 8 7 6 5 4 3 2

Written by Nicholas V. Flammia

Text   1–887744–84–3

TABLE OF CONTENTS

INTRODUCTION

As a teacher of English as a Second Language, I have found the Information Gap technique to be one of the most engaging, motivating, and effective methods for providing students with the opportunity to practice vocabulary and to communicate in content areas. The technique provides for a dynamic exchange of language and for the practice of content vocabulary and concepts within a controlled, communicative setting. The Information Gap activities in this book are ideal for students at all levels of language acquisition, and are a perfect supplement to a content area model of ESL instruction. In fact, any classroom teacher seeking to provide students with the opportunity to utilize academic language will find this book a valuable resource.

ESL Information Gap Activities in the Content Areas provides 25 reproducible Information Gap activities. These activities cover various content topics in Math, Science, Social Studies, and Language Arts and are intended for students from upper elementary grades on up to adults.

HOW DOES AN INFORMATION GAP ACTIVITY WORK?

After the teacher develops concepts, introduces vocabulary, and discusses language structures, each Information Gap activity requires that a pair of students (or a teacher and a student) work together to complete a given task. These tasks can take the form of lists, charts, maps, puzzles, or diagrams. Partners in the pair are labeled "Partner A" and "Partner B" and are provided with corresponding activity sheets that are also labeled A and B.

Partner A possesses information on his sheet that Partner B needs for the activity and Partner B possesses information on his sheet that Partner A needs for the activity. The partners are not permitted to see each other's activity sheets. (I have found that a file folder propped up in between the two partners is an inexpensive, portable, and effective way to provide a barrier for my students.) This creates a gap in each student's information, and thus the term "Information Gap."

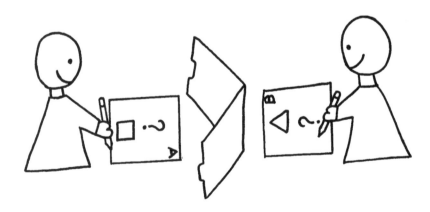

In order for the tasks to be completed, students must exchange information with their partner. The students alternate in the role of speaker 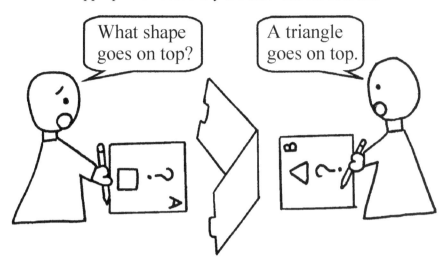 and listener . Communication and utilization of the appropriate vocabulary are essential for success.

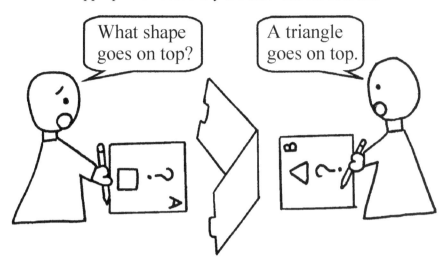

When the students are finished, a comparison of their activity sheets will provide students with the confirmation that they communicated appropriately. If not, students must determine which errors led them to not complete their task successfully. Was it that one partner did not understand a vocabulary term? Was it that he did not phrase a question appropriately? Should the listener have asked for clarification from the speaker?

HOW IS THIS BOOK SET UP?

Before each activity, the teacher will find a list of the targeted content area, the targeted vocabulary, and the targeted language structures. This is followed by step–by–step directions for the teacher to follow. Finally, where appropriate, a follow–up writing activity that utilizes the targeted language is suggested.

ESL INFORMATION GAP ACTIVITIES

CONTENT: Science – Animals – Habitats

VOCABULARY:

Prepositions:	in, on, under, up, at the bottom, to the right of, to the left of, between, above, over
Animal names:	snake, goat, bear, butterfly, duck, ant, deer, squirrel, mouse, frog, gray bird, white bird
Forest vocabulary:	lake, log, mountain, bush, tree, nest, cloud
Verbs:	stand, soar, fly, swim, eat, hide, slither, sit, chirp, walk, crawl, climb

LANGUAGE STRUCTURE:

DIRECTIONS:

–Show the blank picture of the forest and ask students to help label what they see.

–Make a web and ask the students what animals might live in this forest. Add these animal names and add any from the vocabulary that were not mentioned.

–Ask the students to either say or show what each animal might be doing in the forest. Add these verbs to the web.

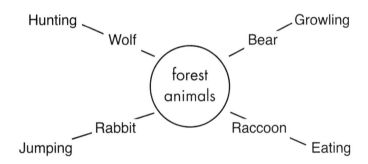

–Use the word bubbles in the Appendix to display the language structures.

–Sketch an animal from the web on the blank forest picture.

–Model the language structures with the web, stressing the *–ing* ending of the verb and the preposition. For example: *What is the rabbit doing? It is jumping over the bush.*

–Sketch other animals in different places on the blank forest picture. Have the students practice asking questions about their locations. Have other students answer with the appropriate vocabulary. Introduce/reinforce the appropriate prepositions when necessary.

*Be certain that students have the opportunity to practice all of the prepositions and verbs in the vocabulary.

INFORMATION GAP:

Have students sit in pairs. Prop open a file folder between the students (or any other barrier that still allows for verbal communication). Hand sheets A to one partner and sheets B to the other.

ANIMALS

Provide the following instructions:

- You have 6 animal pictures in squares.

- You must find where those animals are in your forest picture.

- Use this language (point to the "speaker" and "listener" pictures and questions) to help you.

- Your partner will look at his forest picture and tell you where the animal is and what he is doing.

- Cut your picture out and glue it where it belongs in your forest.

- Take turns asking where your animals go.

- When you are finished, your two forest pictures will look the same.

WRITING FOLLOW–UP:

–Write a paragraph describing your forest scene. <u>Topic sentence:</u> *It's a busy day in the forest.*

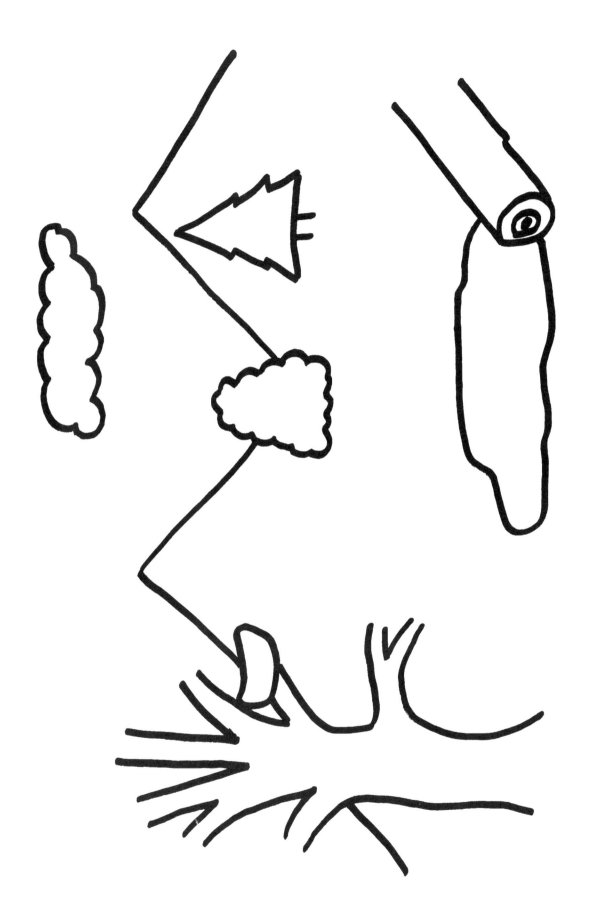

© 2003 NICHOLAS V. FLAMMIA

3

What is the _animal_ doing?

It is _verb_ + ing _where_.

© 2003 NICHOLAS V. FLAMMIA

A

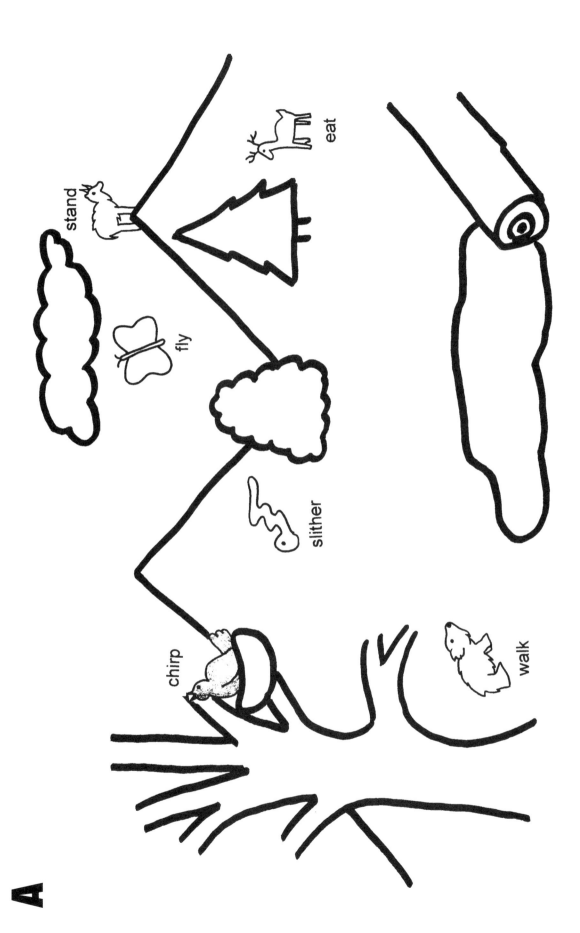

stand

eat

fly

slither

chirp

walk

© 2003 Nicholas V. Flammia

5

What is the _animal_ doing?

It is _verb_ + ing _where_.

© 2003 NICHOLAS V. FLAMMIA

B

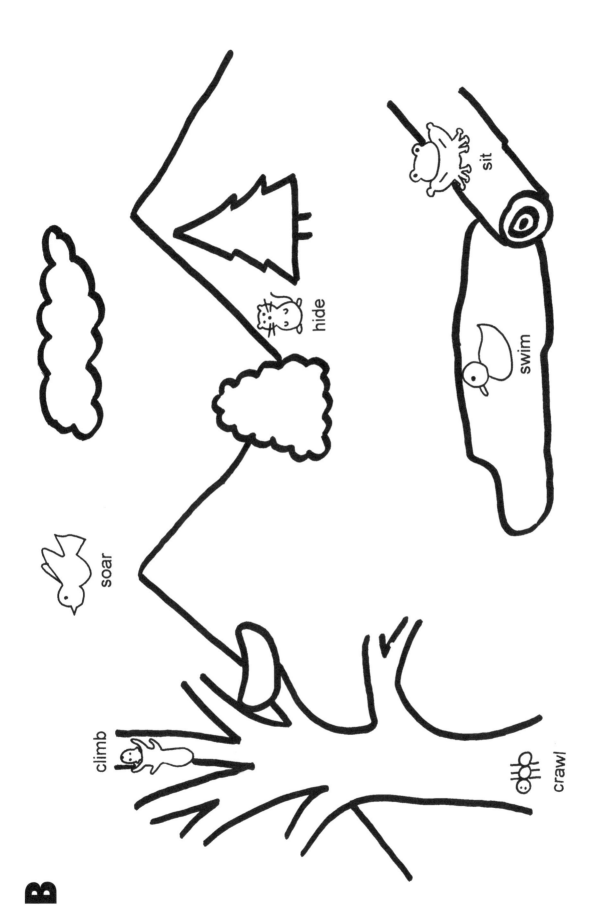

soar

hide

climb

crawl

swim

sit

© 2003 Nicholas V. Flammia

PROPERTIES OF MATTER

CONTENT::   Science – Properties of Matter – Senses

VOCABULARY:

         __Properties:__   words that describe shape, size, taste, color, texture/feel

LANGUAGE STRUCTURE:

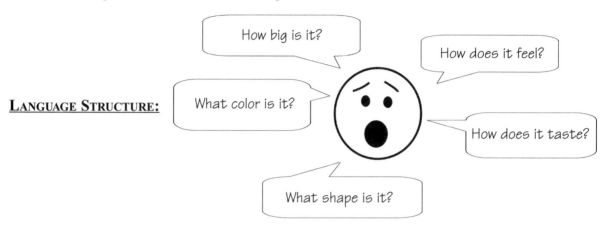

DIRECTIONS:

–Develop vocabulary for shapes, sizes, tastes, colors, and textures. I've done this by walking around the school with students, taking pictures of different objects (they can be drawn by students instead), and mapping out vocabulary for each sense.

–Place a lemon (or other object) in a paper bag and have one student volunteer come up and look at it. This can also be done with a picture of an object.

–Present a copy of the language structures on an overhead projector (or use the word bubbles in the Appendix).

–Have other students try to guess what the "unknown object" in the bag is by asking the student volunteer questions about it's size, shape, taste, color, and feel. Model answers appropriately for the student volunteer.

–Practice with other objects.

INFORMATION GAP:

Have students sit in pairs. Prop open a file folder between the students (or any other barrier that still allows for verbal communication). Hand sheet A to one partner and sheet B to the other.

Provide the following instructions:

● There are 10 "unknown" objects on your chart.

● Take turns asking your partner questions to complete your chart. Begin by saying the number of the unknown object. For example: "Number 5: How big is it?"

● When you're finished, compare your charts.

● Working with your partner, predict what the objects might be. Write this prediction on your charts.

● Then look at your teacher's picture page of objects. Write which object you think it is now. (This page can also be shown on an overhead projector and done as a class activity after all the predictions have been discussed.)

WRITING FOLLOW–UP:

–Write a paragraph describing any object on the chart. Topic sentence: *Have you ever seen a _____?*

–Write a paragraph comparing and contrasting an apple and an orange. Talk about their properties. Topic sentence: *An apple and an orange are both fruits.*

 *ESL INFORMATION GAP ACTIVITIES*

PROPERTIES

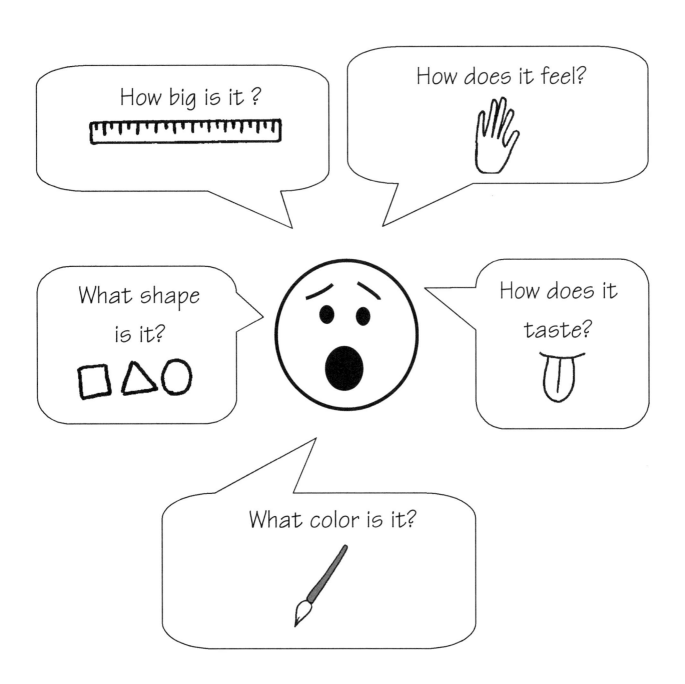

© 2003 Nicholas V. Flammia

Name: _____

Properties – A

DIRECTIONS: Ask your partner for the missing properties.

	SIZE	SHAPE	COLOR	FEEL	TASTE	PREDICTION	OBJECT
1	large	irregular	gray	hard rough			
2	small	rectangular		smooth hard			
3	small	round	orange	bumpy	sweet		
4	small	oval	brown				
5	huge		It comes in many colors.	smooth			
6		oval	green	hard crunchy	sweet		
7	small	rectangular	brown		sweet		
8	small		yellow	hard sharp			
9	large	rectangular	clear	smooth hard			
10	tiny	round		hard smooth	sweet		

© 2003 NICHOLAS V. FLAMMIA

Properties – B

Name: _____

DIRECTIONS: Ask your partner for the missing properties.

	SIZE	SHAPE	COLOR	FEEL	TASTE	PREDICTION	OBJECT
1	tiny	irregular		hard rough	✗		
2	large	square	usually white	smooth hard	✗		
3	small	round	orange		sweet		
4	small		brown	hard rough	sweet		
5		irregular	It comes in many colors.	smooth	✗		
6	big	oval	green		sweet		
7	small		brown	hard crunchy	sweet		
8		cylindrical	yellow	hard sharp	✗		
9	large	rectangular		smooth hard	✗		
10	tiny	round	It comes in many colors.	hard smooth			

© 2003 NICHOLAS V. FLAMMIA

pebble

watermelon

refrigerator

window

pencil

pineapple

car

orange

candy

chocolate bar

© 2003 NICHOLAS V. FLAMMIA

CONTENT: Social Studies – Famous Women

VOCABULARY:

5 Ws: who, what, where, when, why

LANGUAGE STRUCTURE:

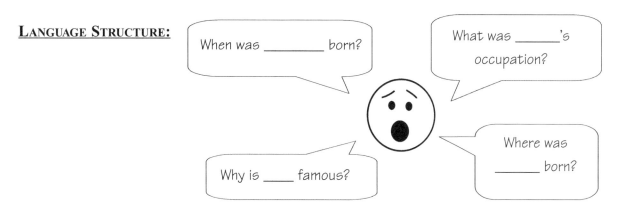

When was _____ born?

What was _____'s occupation?

Where was _____ born?

Why is ____ famous?

DIRECTIONS:

–Show a picture of a famous woman (a person that they are not familiar with works best) and solicit a definition for "famous". Ask students to brainstorm questions that they might have about this person. Point out the importance of the who, what, where, when, and why words in their questions.

– Present a copy of the language structures on an overhead projector (or use the word bubbles in the Appendix).

–Tell them the woman's name. Have students practice asking you the questions about the person. Answer their questions as they practice.

–After you are sure they know the information, ask them the questions and have them answer.

–Have students ask each other about this woman.

INFORMATION GAP

Have students sit in pairs. Prop open a file folder between the students (or any other barrier that still allows for verbal communication). Hand sheet A to one partner and sheet B to the other.

Provide the following instructions:

● This is a chart. It gives information about 5 famous women. (Explain what the headings mean.)

● Take turns asking your partner questions to complete your chart.

● When you are finished, compare your charts.

WRITING FOLLOW–UP:

–Write a paragraph about one of the famous women on the chart. Use information from the completed activity.

–Students may then research another famous woman, find answers to the 5 Ws, and write a paragraph.

FAMOUS WOMEN

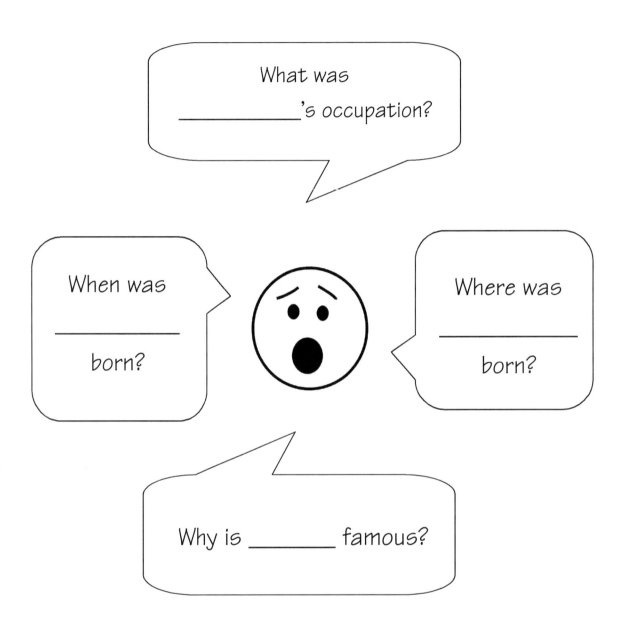

© 2003 NICHOLAS V. FLAMMIA

Name: _____

Famous Women – A

Name	Occupation	Birthplace	Date of Birth	Claim to Fame
Helen Keller	Author – a person that writes books		June 27, 1880	
Jane Goodall		England		researched chimpanzees
Rosa Parks	Seamstress – a person that sews		February 4, 1913	
Amelia Earhart		Kansas		was the first woman to fly by herself across the Atlantic Ocean
Sally Ride			May 26, 1951	was the first American woman to fly into space

© 2003 Nicholas V. Flammia

Name: _____

Famous Women - B

NAME	OCCUPATION	BIRTHPLACE	DATE OF BIRTH	CLAIM TO FAME
Amelia Earhart	<u>Aviator</u> – a person that flies airplanes		July 24, 1897	
Rosa Parks		Alabama		fought for civil rights
Jane Goodall	<u>Ethologist</u> – a person that studies animals		April 3, 1934	
Sally Ride	<u>Astronaut</u> – a person that trains to fly into outer space	California		
Helen Keller		Alabama		was blind and deaf, yet learned to communicate

© 2003 NICHOLAS V. FLAMMIA

CONTENT: Social Studies – Calendar

VOCABULARY:
Temporal: today, tomorrow, yesterday, day, week
Ordinal: first, second, third, fourth, after, last, next

LANGUAGE STRUCTURE: See page 18. (Hand out a copy to students.)

DIRECTIONS:
–Display a calendar, opened to the current month. Write "Today" on the appropriate date's box.
–Select pictures that symbolize <u>special days</u> (such as a birthday cake for a birthday, or an X for a day off from school) and pictures to symbolize <u>actions</u> (such as a book for studying, or a broom for cleaning). Place the pictures with double–stick tape in boxes throughout the month.

– Have students refer to the language structure handout. Looking at where the pictures are situated on the calendar, model asking when actions occurred or will occur. Examples: "When did you study?" "When will you study?"
–Model asking when special days were or when they will be during the month. Examples: "When was your birthday?" Or "When will your birthday be?"

–Explain that we often refer to these occasions in relation to today, without telling the exact date. Use the language structure handout in order to develop the appropriate temporal language to answer the "when questions" (or use the word bubbles in the Appendix).
–Have students practice asking questions and answering them, following the language structure handout.

INFORMATION GAP
Have students sit in pairs. Prop open a file folder between the students (or any other barrier that still allows for verbal communication). Hand sheet A to one partner and sheet B to the other.

Provide the following instructions:

- In front of you there is a calendar. The events on the calendar tell what <u>your</u> special days are and the things that <u>you</u> did or will do this month.

- You must find out about your partner. When do the actions and special days on his calendar take place?

- Look at the squares at the bottom of your calendar. Ask your partner when it happened or will happen. Pay attention to the "past" or "future" labels on top. They will help you ask your question.

- When your partner gives you the answer, cut and paste that square where it belongs on your calendar.

- Take turns asking and answering questions.

- When you are finished, compare your calendars. Are they the same?

WRITING FOLLOW–UP:
–Tell students to imagine that the calendar from the activity describes their month. Have them write a paragraph telling about all that is going on. <u>Topic sentence:</u> *I have a lot happening this month.*
–Make sure the students use information from the calendar and use the temporal language that was practiced.

ESL INFORMATION GAP ACTIVITIES

17

CALENDAR

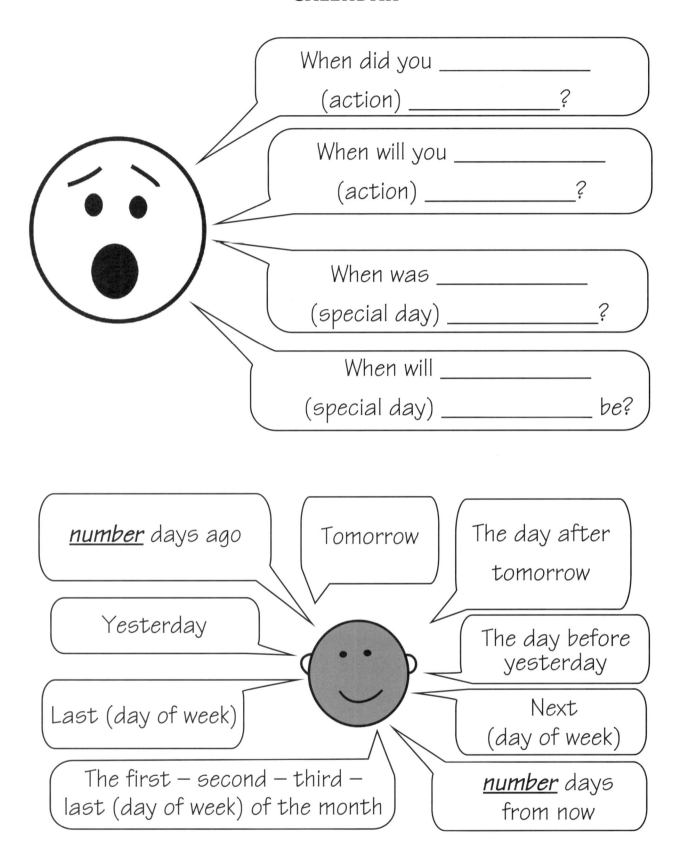

When did you _____
(action) _____?

When will you _____
(action) _____?

When was _____
(special day) _____?

When will _____
(special day) _____ be?

number days ago

Tomorrow

The day after tomorrow

Yesterday

The day before yesterday

Last (day of week)

Next (day of week)

The first – second – third – last (day of week) of the month

number days from now

© 2003 NICHOLAS V. FLAMMIA

Name: _____

Calendar – A

SUNDAY	MONDAY	TUESDAY	WEDNESDAY	THURSDAY	FRIDAY	SATURDAY
				Buy books		
	Sara's birthday		Go see a movie			
			TODAY		Meet with Henry	
		Trip to the museum			First day of vacation	

Find:

Past:	Future:	Past:	Future:	Future:	Past:
Maria's birthday	Do your report	Go shopping	Jose's birthday	Meet with the teacher	The first day of school

© 2003 NICHOLAS V. FLAMMIA

Name: _____ **Calendar – B**

SUNDAY	MONDAY	TUESDAY	WEDNESDAY	THURSDAY	FRIDAY	SATURDAY
		Maria's birthday				
	First day of school					
	Meet with the teacher	Go shopping	Jose's birthday			
		TODAY				Do report

Find:

Past:	Future:	Past:	Future:	Future:	Past:
Go see a movie	The first day of vacation	Sara's birthday	Meet with Henry	The trip to the museum	Buy books

© 2003 Nicholas V. Flammia

LAND AND WATER FEATURES

VOCABULARY:

Land and Water   mountain, volcano, hill, plateau, valley, canyon, plain,
Features: peninsula, river, lake, bay, waterfall, island
Social Studies: latitude and longitude, degrees

LANGUAGE STRUCTURE:
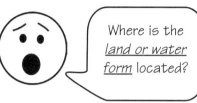

DIRECTIONS:
–Demonstrate how a physical map or globe shows that land and water come in many forms. Make two webs and have students contribute any land or water features that they might know. Add forms from the vocabulary that were not mentioned. Describe and discuss them as a class.

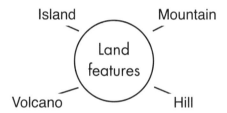
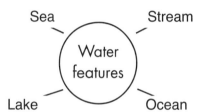

–Show students the latitude and longitude lines on the map or globe and demonstrate how they are used to determine location.
–Practice finding mountain ranges, islands, lakes, etc. on the map and asking students to give its location using the language structures above (or use the word bubbles in the Appendix).

INFORMATION GAP
Have students sit in pairs. Prop open a file folder between the students (or any other barrier that still allows for verbal communication). Hand sheets A to one partner and sheets B to the other.

Provide the following instructions:

● In front of you, you have a map of an island. You also have some land and water features to cut out and place on your island. (Go over the Land and Water Features Key with the students.)

● Take turns asking where your features are located.

● Cut and glue them where they belong.

● When you are finished, compare your grids. Do your islands look the same?

Land and Water Features Key

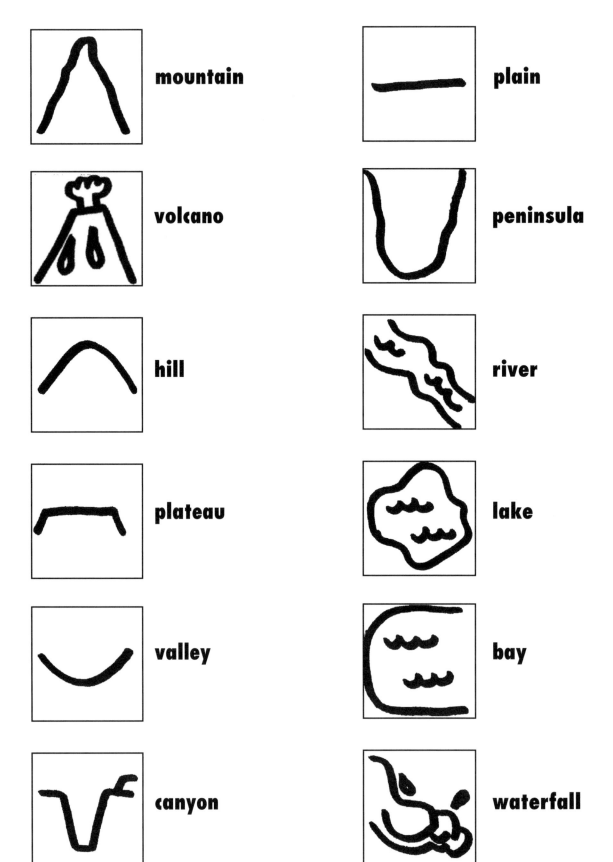

mountain

plain

volcano

peninsula

hill

river

plateau

lake

valley

bay

canyon

waterfall

© 2003 Nicholas V. Flammia

Where is the
_____ located?

It is located at
number degrees *direction*,
number degrees *direction*.

© 2003 Nicholas V. Flammia

© 2003 Nicholas V. Flammia

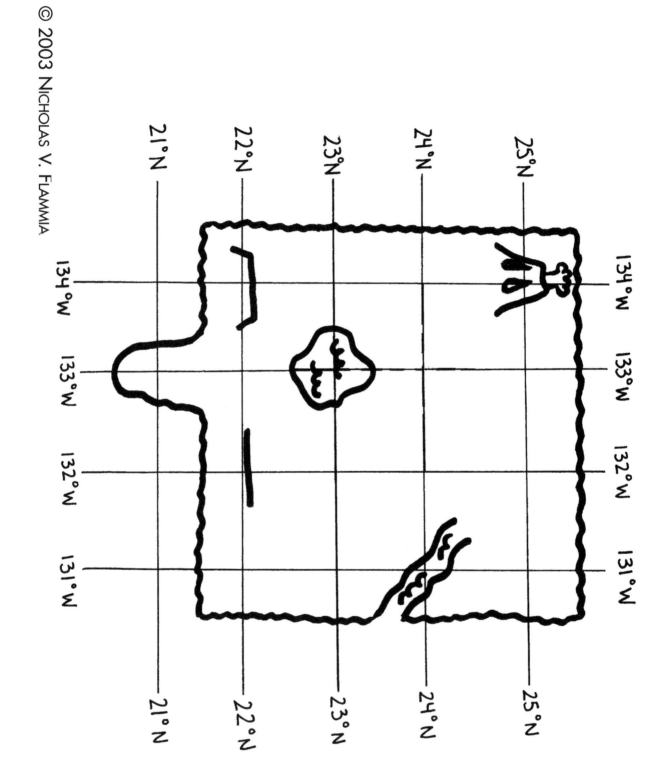

25°N
24°N
23°N
22°N
21°N

134°W
133°W
132°W
131°W

25°N
24°N
23°N
22°N
21°N

1-A

Where is the
_____ located?

It is located at
number degrees *direction*,
number degrees *direction*.

© 2003 NICHOLAS V. FLAMMIA

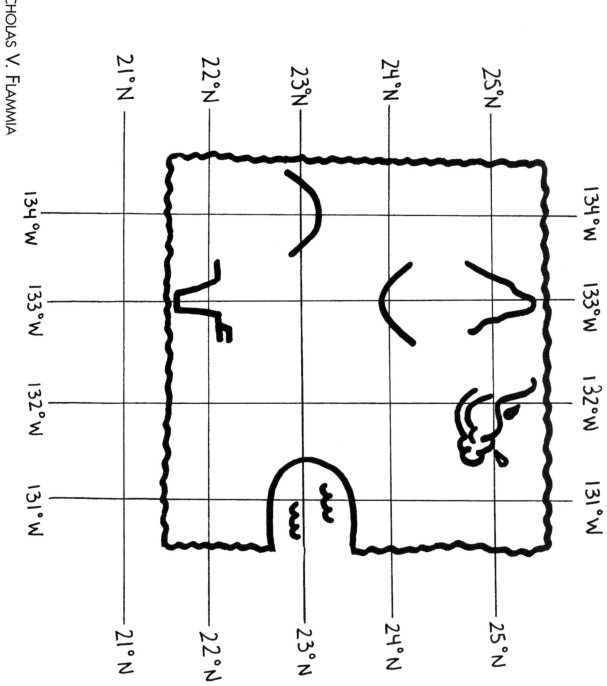

© 2003 Nicholas V. Flammia

1-B

Where is the
_____ located?

It is located at
number degrees *direction*,
number degrees *direction*.

© 2003 NICHOLAS V. FLAMMIA

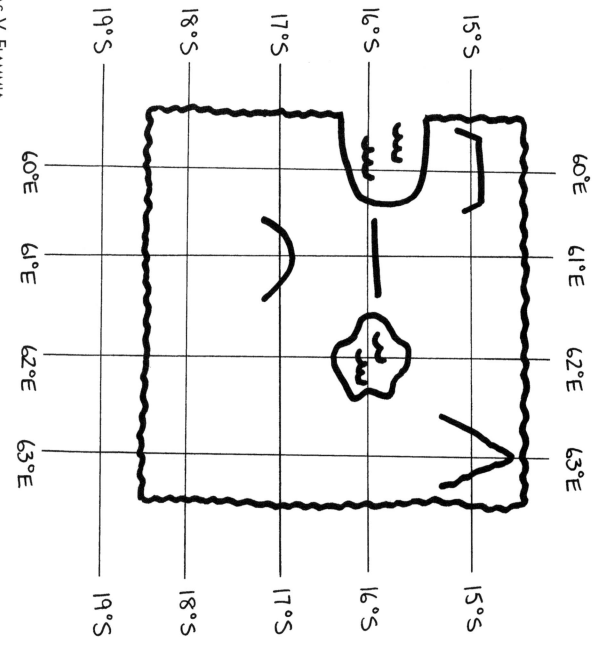

© 2003 Nicholas V. Flammia

2 – A

Where is the
_____ located?

It is located at
number degrees *direction*,
number degrees *direction*.

© 2003 Nicholas V. Flammia

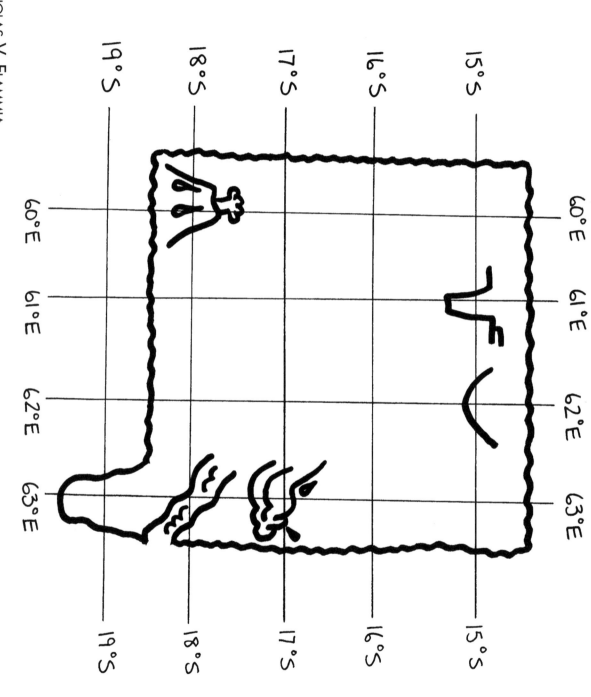

© 2003 Nicholas V. Flammia

15°S
16°S
17°S
18°S
19°S

60°E
61°E
62°E
63°E

15°S
16°S
17°S
18°S
19°S

2 – B

CONTENT: Social Studies – Community

VOCABULARY:

City: blocks, supermarket, movie theatre, school, hotel, hardware store, toy store, shoe store, department store, restaurant, museum, firehouse, police station

Direction concepts: go straight, turn left, turn right, on the left, on the right

Location concepts: first on the right/left, second on the right/left

LANGUAGE STRUCTURE:

How can I get to the **place**?

DIRECTIONS:

–Ask students to name a city that they know.

–With student contributions, make a web of the places and stores that are in a city. Add any of the "City" vocabulary that was not mentioned by students.

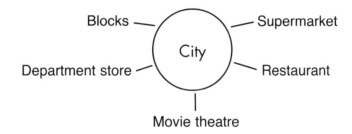

–Ask students if they can tell you how they would travel to any one of the places on the web from their school. Introduce "Direction" and "Location" concepts as they do this.

–Have students arrange their desks into "city blocks". Assign a student a place name. Ask the class, "How can I get to the *place*?" Have students give you directions. Reinforce vocabulary.

INFORMATION GAP

Have the students sit in pairs. Prop open a file folder between the students (or any other barrier that still allows for verbal communication). Hand sheet A to one partner and sheet B to the other.

Provide the following instructions:

● You have a map of a city.

● You must find where the places at the bottom of the map are in this city.

● Your partner will look at his map and tell you how to get there from the arrow at the bottom.

● Cut the squares out and glue them where they belong.

● Take turns.

● When you are finished, your two city maps should look the same.

WRITING FOLLOW–UP:

–Write a paragraph telling a tourist how to get to the hotel, the museum, and the movie theatre. Use the city map from the information gap activity as a reference. Topic sentence: *It's easy for visitors to get around in this city.*

Name_____ **City A**

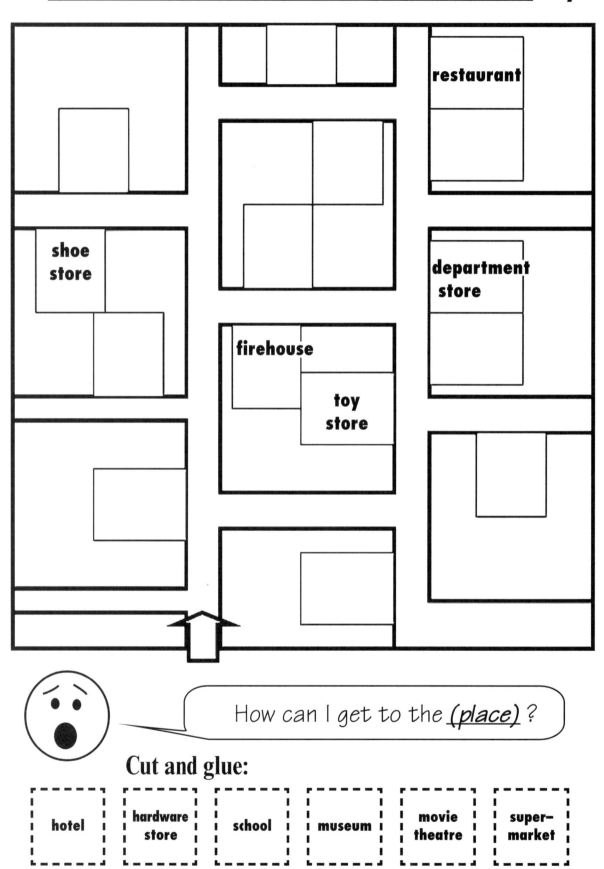

restaurant

shoe store

department store

firehouse

toy store

How can I get to the *(place)* ?

Cut and glue:

| hotel | hardware store | school | museum | movie theatre | super-market |

32   © 2003 Nᴵᴄʜᴏʟᴀs V. Fʟᴀᴍᴍɪᴀ

school

super-
market

hotel

museum

hardware
store

movie
theatre

How can I get to the *(place)* ?

Cut and glue:

| shoe store | restaurant | firehouse | department store | police station | toy store |

© 2003 Nicholas V. Flammia

COLONIAL VILLAGE

<u>CONTENT:</u>   Social Studies – Colonial Times – Colonial Villages

<u>VOCABULARY:</u>

<u>Colonial Village:</u> tannery, inn, schoolhouse, blacksmith, grist mill, meetinghouse, cooper, cobbler, potter, general store, chandlery, printer

<u>Direction concepts:</u> go straight, make a left, make a right

<u>Location concepts:</u> first (second, third, etc.) on the right/left

<u>LANGUAGE STRUCTURE:</u>

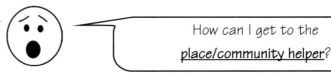

How can I get to the *place/community helper?*

<u>DIRECTIONS:</u>

During a unit on colonial times, introduce the different places and community helpers that existed in colonial villages. Make a T–list explaining what these places and community helpers were and what their functions were.

Example:

Place/Community Helper	Function
tanner	made leather from animal skins in order to make shoes, work aprons, belts, and saddles

–Have students arrange their desks to simulate the buildings of a colonial village. Assign a student a place/community helper name (such as blacksmith). Ask the class, "How can I get to *place/community helper*?" Have students give you directions. Reinforce vocabulary.

INFORMATION GAP

Have the students sit in pairs. Prop open a file folder between the students (or any other barrier that still allows for verbal communication). Hand sheet A to one partner and sheet B to the other.

Provide the following instructions:

● You have a map of a colonial village.

● You must find where the places and community helpers at the bottom of the map are in this colonial village.

● Your partner will look at his map and tell you how to get there from the arrow at the bottom.

● Cut the squares out and glue them where they belong.

● Take turns.

● When you are finished, your two colonial village maps should look the same.

WRITING FOLLOW–UP:

Write a paragraph contrasting a modern city and a colonial village. Use contrasting words such as but, while, whereas, yet, and however. <u>Topic sentence:</u> *A colonial village was different from today's modern city.*

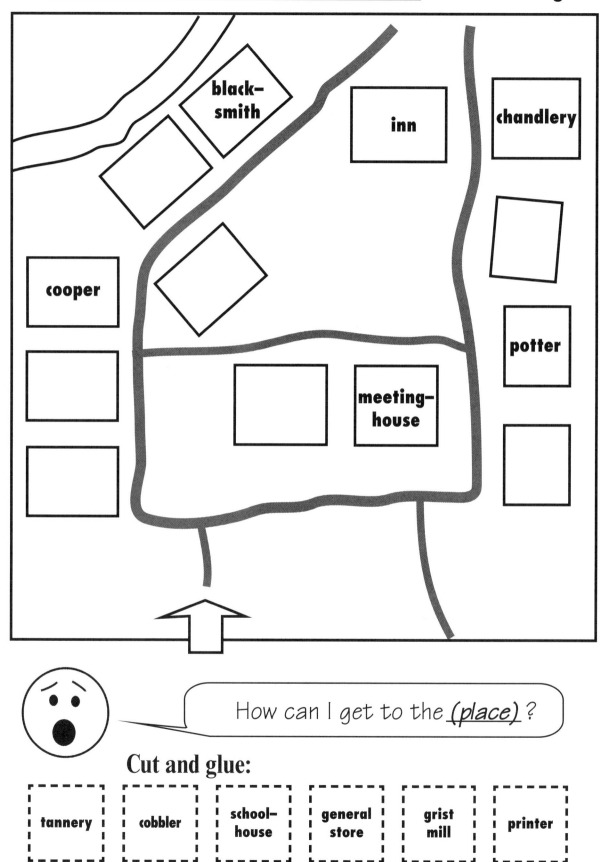

How can I get to the *(place)* ?

Cut and glue:

tannery | cobbler | school-house | general store | grist mill | printer

© 2003 NICHOLAS V. FLAMMIA

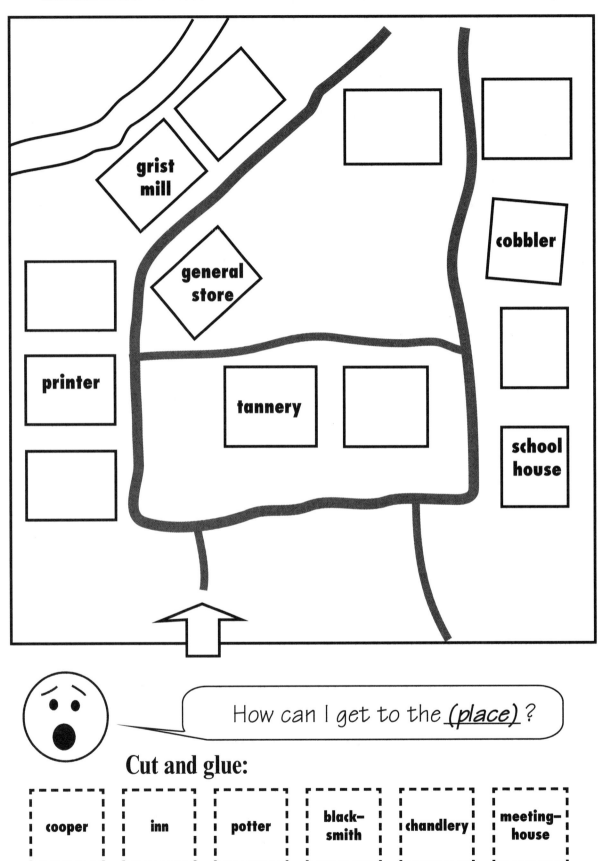

grist mill

general store

cobbler

printer

tannery

school house

How can I get to the *(place)*?

Cut and glue:

cooper | inn | potter | black-smith | chandlery | meeting-house

© 2003 NICHOLAS V. FLAMMIA

CONTENT: Math – Coordinates

VOCABULARY:
    Items in a House: bathtub, sink, toilet, refrigerator, microwave oven, table, couch/sofa, lamp, television, bed, dresser, nightstand
    Math: coordinate, grid

LANGUAGE STRUCTURE:

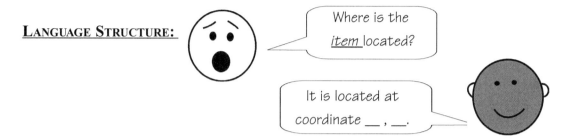

DIRECTIONS:
–Write "house" in a circle and branch off the names of rooms in a house. Ask students what may be found in these rooms and add any student contributions to the web. Add any items not listed from the vocabulary list. Example:

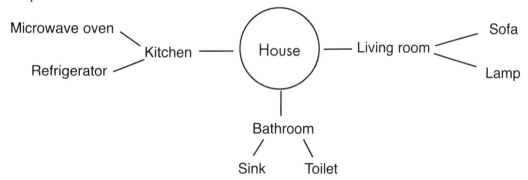

–Show a grid and explain that a grid helps us to locate items by identifying exact points. Number the grid and explain that each place where two lines meet is called a "coordinate."
–Put a picture (or draw a picture) of any household item on the grid and ask, "Where is the _____ located?" Have students answer with the sentence, "It is located at coordinate __, __." (Word bubbles in the Appendix can be used to display the language structures.)
–Give students practice asking and giving coordinates for any other items that are added to the grid.

INFORMATION GAP
Have the students sit in pairs. Prop open a file folder between the students (or any other barrier that still allows for verbal communication). Hand sheet A to one partner and sheet B to the other.

Provide the following instructions:

● You have a grid in front of you. Some items are on your grid. Others are on your partner's grid.

● Ask your partner where the items at the bottom are located.

● Draw them where they belong.

● Take turns asking for where your items are located.

● When you are finished, compare your grids.

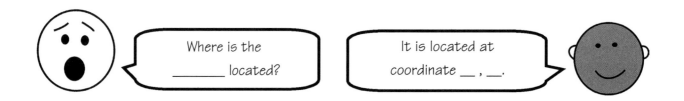

Where is the _____ located?

It is located at coordinate __ , __.

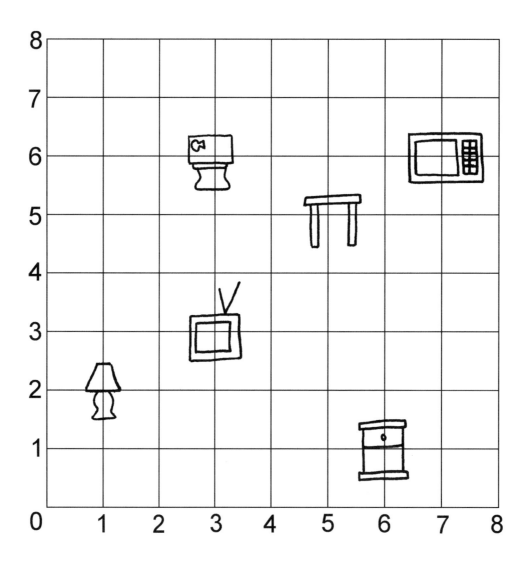

Find:

© 2003 NICHOLAS V. FLAMMIA

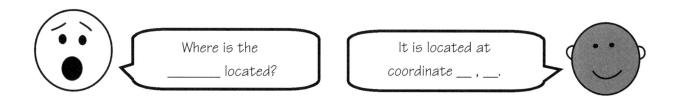

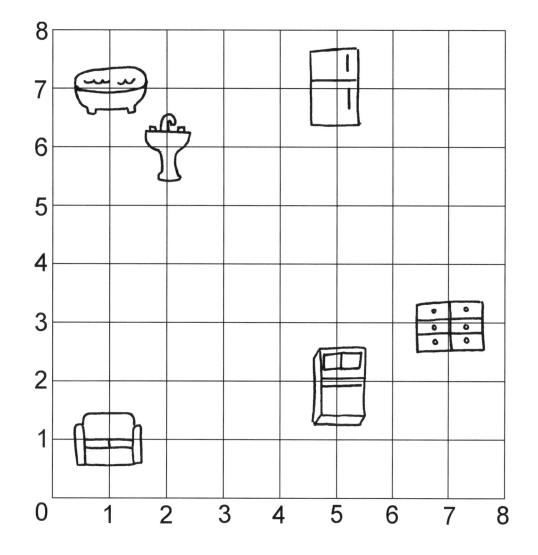

Find:

© 2003 Nicholas V. Flammia

UNITED STATES

VOCABULARY:

   Cardinal Directions: north, south, east, west

Intermediate Directions: northwest, northeast, southwest, southeast

   Geography: names of states in the continental United States

LANGUAGE STRUCTURE:

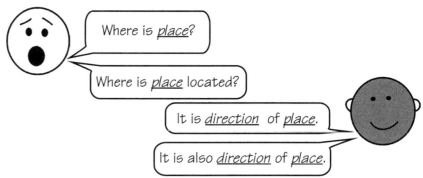

Where is *place*?

Where is *place* located?

It is *direction* of *place*.

It is also *direction* of *place*.

DIRECTIONS:

–Display a map and point out the compass rose. Explain how the compass rose indicates direction on the map. (Refer to the cardinal and intermediate directions in the vocabulary.)

–Present a copy of the language structures on an overhead projector (or use the word bubbles in the Appendix) and model asking for location and telling location. Example:

> Where is Minnesota?

> It is east of North Dakota. It is also west of Wisconsin.

–Have student volunteers practice asking the class for the location of other places on the map.

–Explain to students that each state in the United States has a two letter abbreviation. Display the "State Abbreviations and Names" key on an overhead projector, hand out a copy to each student, or rewrite it on a chart for all the students to see.

–Tell students that today they are going to locate these states on a map using cardinal directions and intermediate directions.

INFORMATION GAP

Have the students sit in pairs. Prop open a file folder between the students (or any other barrier that still allows for verbal communication). Hand sheet A to one partner and sheet B to the other.

Provide the following instructions:

● You and your partner have maps of the continental United States.

● On top of your map are the abbreviations of states that you must find.

● Ask your partner for their locations in the order that they are listed.

● When your partner tells you where a state is located, write its abbreviation on your map.

● If you can't find it, ask for more information

● Take turns.

● When you are finished, your teacher will give you instructions on how to color your map.

● Compare your map with your partner's map. Do the colors match?

 *ESL INFORMATION GAP ACTIVITIES*

WRITING FOLLOW–UP:

–Write a paragraph about the location of any one state. Use the language structures practiced today.

–Possible topic sentences: _State's name_ is one of the 50 states.

State's name is bordered by _number_ states.

–Detail sentences tell its relative location. For example: It is south of _another state_. It is also north of _another state_. It is east of _another state_ and west of _another state_.

STATE ABBREVIATIONS & NAMES

A

AL	Alabama
AZ	Arizona
AR	Arkansas

C

CA	California
CO	Colorado
CT	Connecticut

D

DE	Delaware

F

FL	Florida

G

GA	Georgia

I

ID	Idaho
IL	Illinois
IN	Indiana
IA	Iowa

K

KS	Kansas
KY	Kentucky

L

LA	Louisiana

M

ME	Maine
MD	Maryland
MA	Massachusetts
MI	Michigan
MN	Minnesota
MS	Mississippi
MO	Missouri
MT	Montana

N

NE	Nebraska
NV	Nevada
NH	New Hampshire
NJ	New Jersey
NM	New Mexico
NY	New York
NC	North Carolina
ND	North Dakota

O

OH	Ohio
OK	Oklahoma
OR	Oregon

P

PA	Pennsylvania

R

RI	Rhode Island

S

SC	South Carolina
SD	South Dakota

T

TN	Tennessee
TX	Texas

U

UT	Utah

V

VT	Vermont
VA	Virginia

W

WA	Washington
WV	West Virginia
WI	Wisconsin
WY	Wyoming

© 2003 NICHOLAS V. FLAMMIA

UNITED STATES

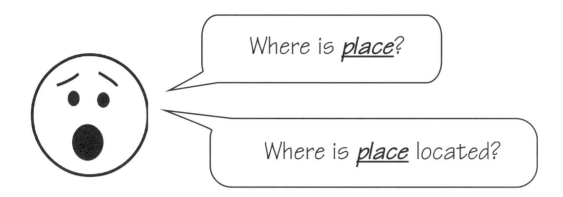

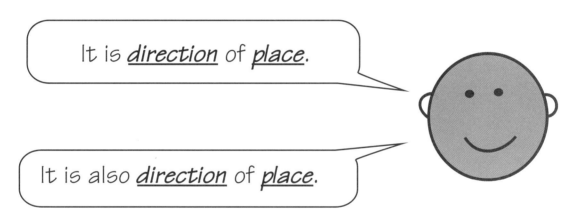

© 2003 Nicholas V. Flammia

Find:

United States – A

NE	TX	CO	WY	ND	ID	CA	MO	KY	NY	ME	MS	IL	OH	VA	MD	RI	SC

© 2003 Nicholas V. Flammia

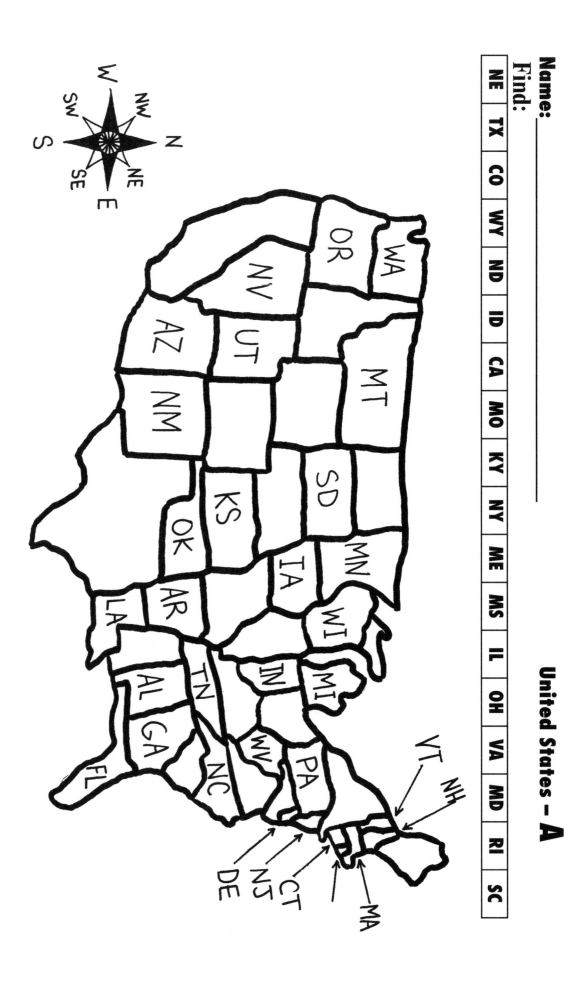

44

United States – **B**

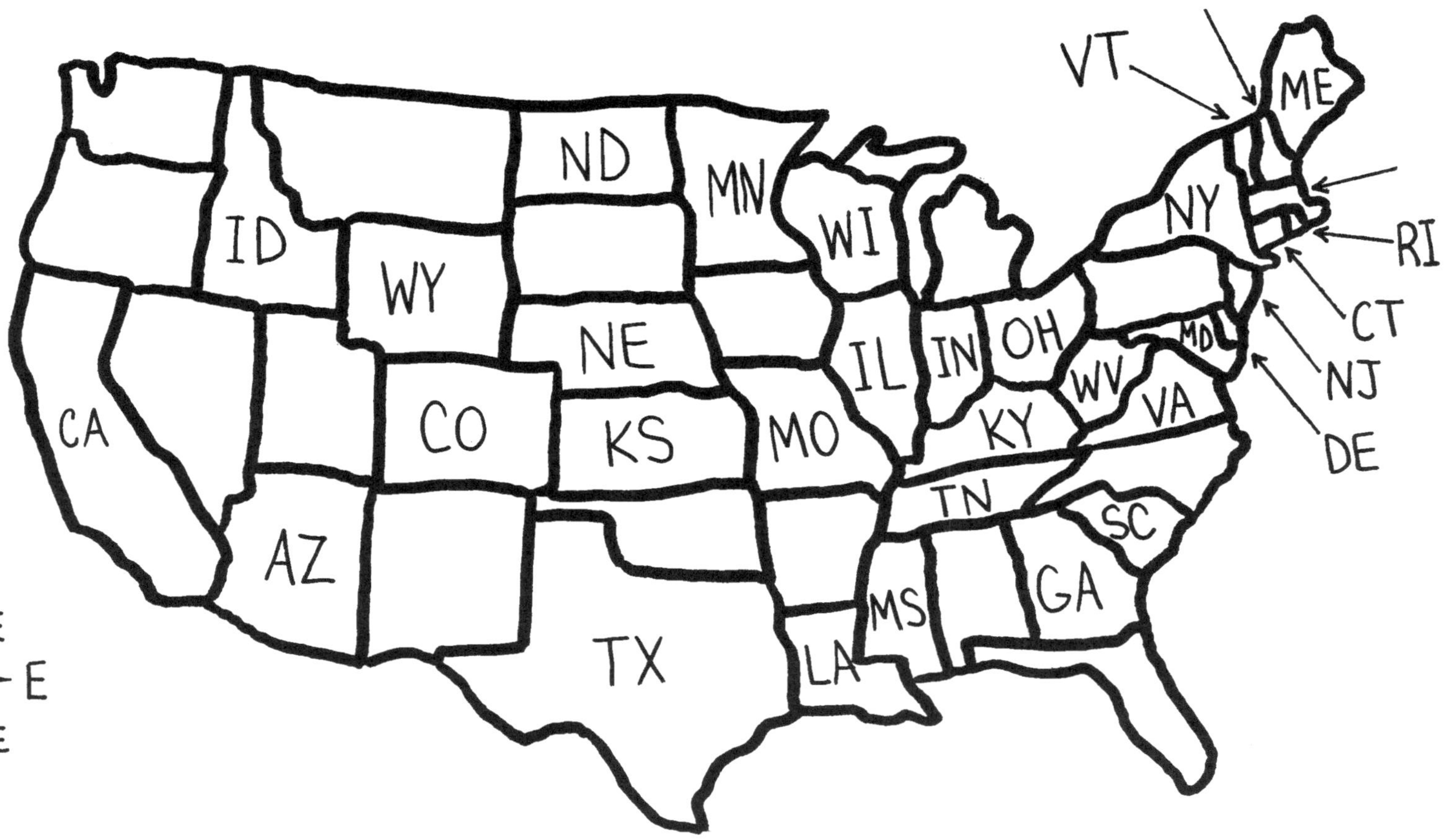

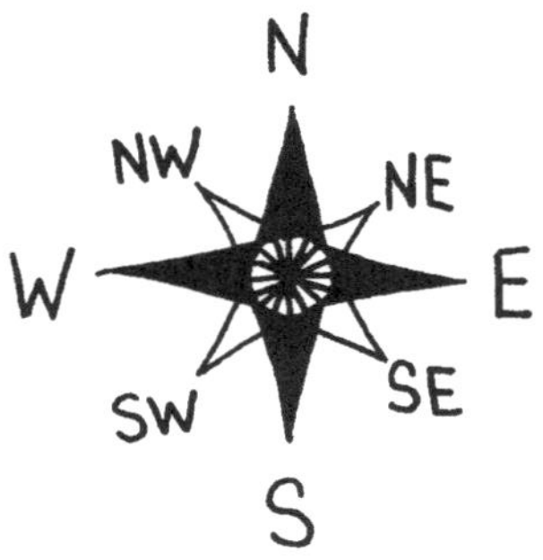

© 2003 Nicholas V. Flammia

DIRECTIONS:

Color the states on your map.

Look at the first letter in the state's name.

The key below will tell you which color to use.

When finished, compare your map with your partner's map.

KEY

If it begins with A or P	→	Color it RED.
If it begins with C or R	→	Color it ORANGE.
If it begins with D or V	→	Color it WHITE.
If it begins with N	→	Color it YELLOW.
If it begins with F or O	→	Color it GREEN.
If it begins with G or W	→	Color it DARK BLUE.
If it begins with I or U	→	Color it PURPLE.
If it begins with K or T	→	Color it PINK.
If it begins with L or S	→	Color it BROWN.
If it begins with M	→	Color it LIGHT BLUE.

© 2003 NICHOLAS V. FLAMMIA

CONTENT: Math – Place Value Reading – Numbers

VOCABULARY:
        Numbers: hundred, thousand, million
        Directions: match

LANGUAGE STRUCTURE:

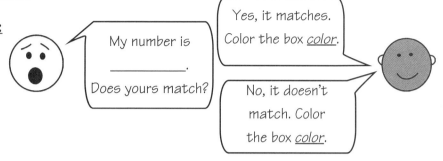

DIRECTIONS:

Activity I

–Teach students to recognize numbers up to the hundred's place. Then do Activity I following the instructions below.

 Input: Say "hundred" after the hundred's place. Then read the ten's and one's places together. Example:

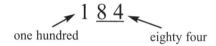

$$\nearrow 1\ \underline{8\ 4} \nwarrow$$

one hundred   eighty four

Activity II

–Teach students to recognize numbers up to the hundred thousand's place. Then do Activity II following the instructions below.

 Input: Read the numbers before the comma as above. Say "thousand" when you see the comma. Then read the rest of the number. Example:

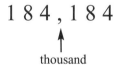

1 8 4 , 1 8 4

↑
thousand

Activity III

–Teach students to recognize numbers up to the hundred million's place. Then do Activity III following the instructions below.

 Input: Read the numbers before the comma. Say "million" when you see the first comma. Read the next set of numbers as before, saying "thousand" at the next comma. Then read the rest of the numbers as before.

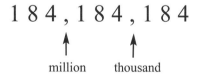

1 8 4 , 1 8 4 , 1 8 4

↑   ↑
million   thousand

* Remember to alert students not to say "thousand" when there are all zeros in the hundred thousand's, the ten thousand's, and the thousand's places. Example: 184,000,184

NUMBERS – ACTIVITIES I – III

→ **Getting Ready for the Activity:** Define the word "match" for your students. Get enough index cards for each student. Write numbers on them so that each card will have a match. For example:

| 10 | 10 | 8 | 8 | 5 | 5 |

Randomly hand one to each student. Present the language structures (or use the word bubbles in the Appendix). Tell the students that they must find another student that has a card with a matching number by using the language structure you provided. Model the language appropriately.

INFORMATION GAP

Have students sit in pairs. Prop open a file folder between the students (or any other barrier that still allows for verbal communication). Hand sheet A to one partner and sheet B to the other.

Be sure to provide students with the colored markers needed. Each student should have a blue and red marker for Activity I, a green and yellow marker for Activity II, and a yellow and orange marker for Activity III.

Provide the following instructions:

● There are 24 squares on your sheet labeled A – X.

● Pick a box. Ask your partner if his number is the same as yours. Say the letter of the box first. For example: "Box A: My number is _____. Does yours match?"

● Your partner will tell you whether your number matches his. He will then give you instructions on how to color that box and color his the same color.

● Take turns asking your partner if his numbers are the same as yours.

● When you are finished, compare your papers. Do they match?

● Check your paper with the teacher's key.

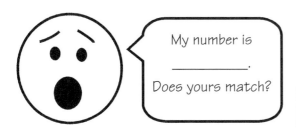

My number is _____. Does yours match?

Yes, it matches. Color the box blue.

No, it doesn't match. Color the box red.

A	B	C	D
120	395	654	800
E	**F**	**G**	**H**
111	268	798	333
I	**J**	**K**	**L**
100	420	399	482
M	**N**	**O**	**P**
550	300	750	220
Q	**R**	**S**	**T**
210	382	908	650
U	**V**	**W**	**X**
518	874	875	988

© 2003 Nicholas V. Flammia

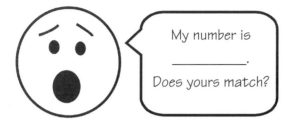

A	B	C	D
120	375	654	800
E	**F**	**G**	**H**
111	628	898	303
I	**J**	**K**	**L**
100	420	309	482
M	**N**	**O**	**P**
560	303	700	222
Q	**R**	**S**	**T**
110	382	980	650
U	**V**	**W**	**X**
518	874	855	588

© 2003 NICHOLAS V. FLAMMIA

NUMBERS – KEY

A	B	C	D
blue	**red**	**blue**	**blue**
E	F	G	H
blue	**red**	**red**	**red**
I	J	K	L
blue	**blue**	**red**	**blue**
M	N	O	P
red	**red**	**red**	**red**
Q	R	S	T
red	**blue**	**red**	**blue**
U	V	W	X
blue	**blue**	**red**	**red**

© 2003 Nicholas V. Flammia

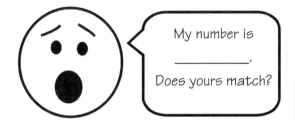

A	B	C	D
45,265	100,265	655,300	5,201
E	F	G	H
29,606	505,505	300,000	20,090
I	J	K	L
44,004	990,009	199,199	265,000
M	N	O	P
49,049	606,166	763,633	865,650
Q	R	S	T
26,560	400,040	16,000	480,009
U	V	W	X
888,080	735,982	263,846	900,560

© 2003 Nicholas V. Flammia

A	**B**	**C**	**D**
45,265	100,265	655,300	52,001
E	**F**	**G**	**H**
29,660	500,505	300,000	20,090
I	**J**	**K**	**L**
44,400	999,000	190,199	265,000
M	**N**	**O**	**P**
49,049	606,166	760,633	865,065
Q	**R**	**S**	**T**
26,560	440,000	106,000	480,009
U	**V**	**W**	**X**
880,008	739,582	263,846	905,060

© 2003 Nicholas V. Flammia

NUMBERS II – KEY

A	B	C	D
green	green	green	yellow
E	**F**	**G**	**H**
yellow	yellow	green	green
I	**J**	**K**	**L**
yellow	yellow	yellow	green
M	**N**	**O**	**P**
green	green	yellow	yellow
Q	**R**	**S**	**T**
green	yellow	yellow	green
U	**V**	**W**	**X**
yellow	yellow	green	yellow

© 2003 NICHOLAS V. FLAMMIA

My number is
_____.
Does yours match?

Yes, it matches.
Color the box orange.

No, it doesn't match.
Color the box yellow.

A	B	C	D
10,000,000	48,048,048	756,056,300	201,100,200
E	**F**	**G**	**H**
4,562,350	40,040,040	980,900,009	22,022,022
I	**J**	**K**	**L**
678,235,020	1,000,000	899,000,100	52,520,000
M	**N**	**O**	**P**
999,990,999	704,800,632	632,006,000	25,000,025
Q	**R**	**S**	**T**
65,100,000	100,100,001	21,001,003	48,700,000
U	**V**	**W**	**X**
330,030,000	5,000,050	956,956,956	645,253,555

© 2003 Nicholas V. Flammia

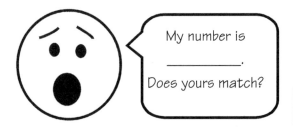

A	B	C	D
1,000,000	40,848,048	756,056,300	200,100,200
E	**F**	**G**	**H**
4,562,350	40,004,040	980,000,909	22,220,022
I	**J**	**K**	**L**
678,205,020	1,000,000	899,000,100	52,520,000
M	**N**	**O**	**P**
990,999,999	704,800,632	632,006,000	25,025,000
Q	**R**	**S**	**T**
605,001,000	100,001,001	21,001,003	48,700,000
U	**V**	**W**	**X**
333,330,000	5,050,000	900,956,956	645,253,555

© 2003 Nicholas V. Flammia

Numbers III – KEY

A yellow	B yellow	C orange	D yellow
E orange	F yellow	G yellow	H yellow
I yellow	J orange	K orange	L orange
M yellow	N orange	O orange	P yellow
Q yellow	R yellow	S orange	T orange
U yellow	V yellow	W yellow	X orange

© 2003 Nicholas V. Flammia

ADDITION AND SUBTRACTION

CONTENT: Math – Addition – Subtraction – Shapes

VOCABULARY:

      Math: plus, minus

      Shapes: square, circle, pentagon, oval, octagon, rhombus, triangle, rectangle, hexagon, trapezoid

LANGUAGE STRUCTURE:

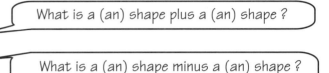

What is a (an) shape plus a (an) shape ?

What is a (an) shape minus a (an) shape ?

DIRECTIONS:

–Make a web with the word "shape" in the middle. Have students contribute the names of shapes that they know. (Draw the shapes and label them as illustrated below.) Add any from the vocabulary that were not included.

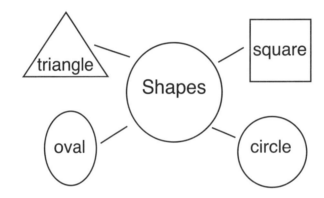

–Have students randomly write one number in each shape.

–Present the language structures using the word bubbles in the Appendix. Make an addition and subtraction equation with two of the shapes and model reading the equation. For example:

What is a square plus a triangle?

–Have students come to the chalkboard, write an equation with the shapes, and then have other students answer them.

INFORMATION GAP

Have the students sit in pairs. Prop open a file folder between the students (or any other barrier that still allows for communication). Hand sheets A to one partner and sheets B to the other.

Provide the following instructions:

● On your first sheet, there is a box. The box has shapes with numbers in them. Your partner has shapes with different numbers than the ones in your shapes.

● You must ask your partner for the answers to the addition and subtraction problems on your sheet.

● Your partner must use the shapes in his box to give you the answers.

● When he gives you an answer, draw a line to that answer on your connect–the–dots page. (Begin where it

says "Start.")

● Make sure you ask your questions in order. Connect each answer on the connect–the–dots page to the previous answer.

● Take turns.

● When you are finished, compare your connect–the–dots pages.

*Modification for younger students:

Have younger students first get all seven answers and record them next to the equations on the question page. Then they can be given the connect–the–dots pages and be instructed to connect their answers in the order that they were given.

Name:_____ **Addition and Subtraction – A**

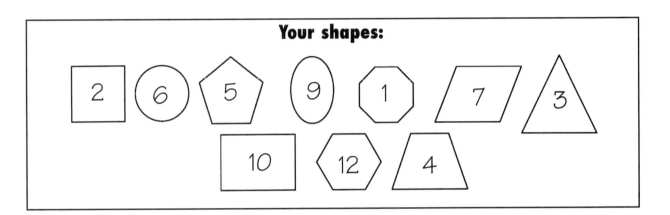

What is a (an) _shape_ plus a (an) _shape_ ?

What is a (an) _shape_ minus a (an) _shape_ ?

Your shapes:

2   6   5   9   1   7   3

10   12   4

Ask your partner:

1. ◯ + △ =

2. ◯ − ☐ =

3. ▱ − ⬠ =

4. ◯ + ▱ =

5. ☐ + ⯃ =

6. ☐ − ⬠ =

7. ▱ − ⬡ =

© 2003 Nicholas V. Flammia

ADDITION AND SUBTRACTION A

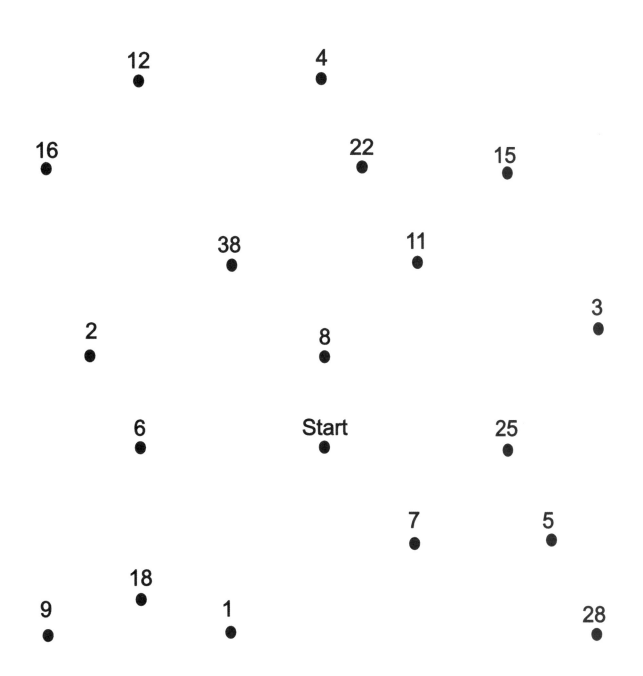

© 2003 NICHOLAS V. FLAMMIA

What is a (an) _shape_ plus a (an) _shape_ ?

What is a (an) _shape_ minus a (an) _shape_ ?

Your shapes:

| 4 | 16 | 3 | 8 | 6 | 7 | 9 |

5 2 12

Ask your partner:

1. ☐ − ☐ =

5. ◯ − ▱ =

2. ▱ + △ =

6. ⬡ + ◯ =

3. ◯ − ☐ =

7. ⬠ + ☐ =

4. ▱ + ☐ =

© 2003 NICHOLAS V. FLAMMIA

Addition and Subtraction B

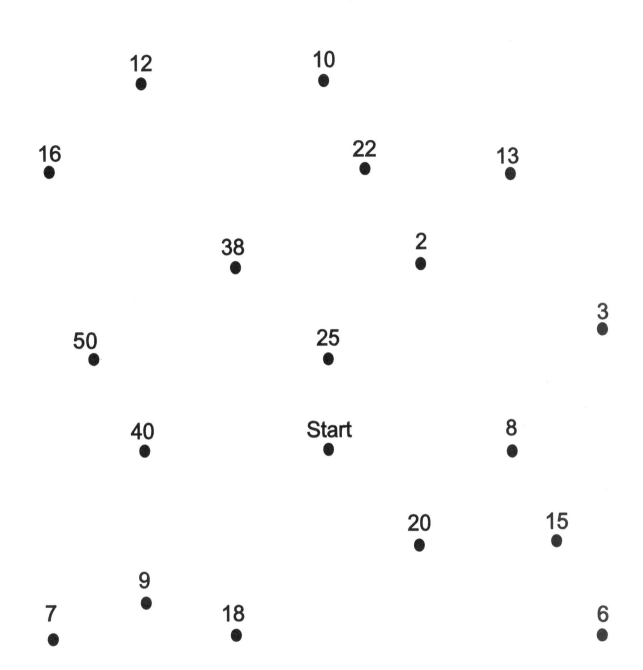

© 2003 Nicholas V. Flammia

MULTIPLICATION AND DIVISION

CONTENT: Math – Multiplication – Division – Shapes

VOCABULARY:

         Math: times, divided by

       Shapes: square, circle, pentagon, oval, octagon, rhombus, triangle, rectangle, hexagon, trapezoid

LANGUAGE STRUCTURE:

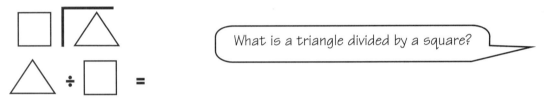

> What is a (an) *shape* times a (an) *shape*?

> What is a (an) *shape* divided by a (an) *shape*?

DIRECTIONS:

–Follow the beginning portion of the previous "addition and subtraction" information gap activity. Set up the web as explained, except, place numbers that will allow for division in the shapes.

–On a chalkboard, set up multiplication and division equations with the shapes. Present the language structures using the word bubbles in the Appendix. Model reading the equations. Make sure you model division examples in both forms. For example:

$$\square \quad \triangle$$

$$\triangle \div \square =$$

> What is a triangle divided by a square?

–Have students come to the chalkboard, write an equation with the shapes, and then have other students answer them.

INFORMATION GAP

Have the students sit in pairs. Prop open a file folder between the students (or any other barrier that still allows for communication). Hand sheets A to one partner and sheets B to the other.

Provide the following instructions:

- On your first sheet, there is a box. The box has shapes with numbers in them. Your partner has shapes with different numbers than the ones in your shapes.

- You must ask your partner for the answers to the multiplication and division problems on your sheet.

- Your partner must use the shapes in his box to give you the answers.

- When he gives you an answer, draw a line to that answer on your connect–the–dots page. (Begin where it says "Start.")

- Make sure you ask your questions in order. Connect each answer on the connect–the–dots page to the previous answer.

- Take turns.

- When you are finished, compare your connect–the–dots pages.

*Modification for younger students:

Have younger students first get all seven answers and record them next to the equations on the question page. Then they can be given the connect–the–dots pages and be instructed to connect their answers in the order that they were given.

What is a (an) _shape_ times a (an) _shape_ ?

What is a (an) _shape_ divided by a (an) _shape_ ?

Your shapes:

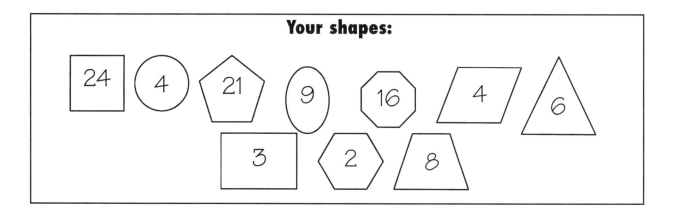

24   4   21   9   16   4   6

3   2   8

Ask your partner:

1. ⬠ × ⬡ =

2. ◯ × ⯃ =

3. ▱ | ⬓

4. ▭ ÷ ⬡ =

5. ▱ × ⬠ =

6. ⯃ | ▢

7. △ × ⬡ =

© 2003 NICHOLAS V. FLAMMIA

MULTIPLICATION AND DIVISION A

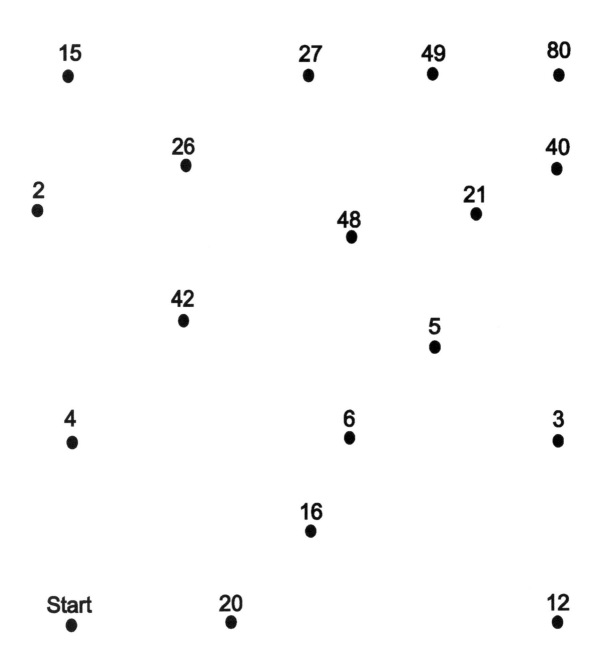

© 2003 NICHOLAS V. FLAMMIA

What is a (an) <u>shape</u> times a (an) <u>shape</u> ?

What is a (an) <u>shape</u> divided by a (an) <u>shape</u> ?

Your shapes:

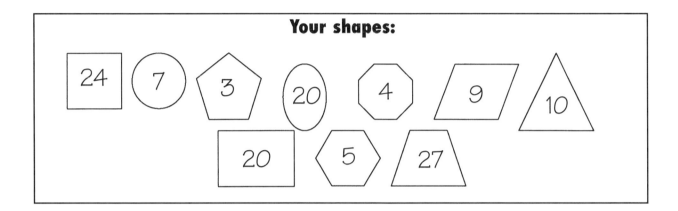

Ask your partner:

1. ☐ × △ =

2. ⬡/⬠

3. ▱ × △ =

4. ⬭ × ◯ =

5. ⬠ ÷ ☐ =

6. ⬡/☐ =

7. ⬠ × ▱ =

© 2003 NICHOLAS V. FLAMMIA

Multiplication and Division B

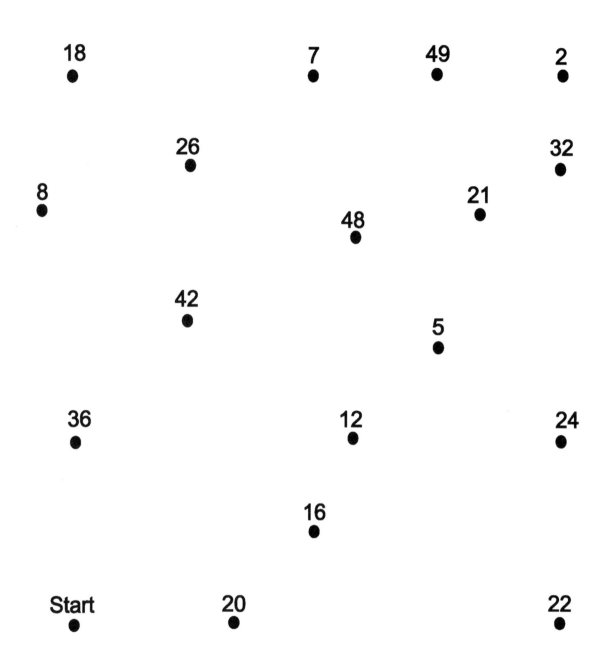

© 2003 Nicholas V. Flammia

MATHEMATICAL LANGUAGE

__CONTENT:__   Math – Addition – Subtraction – Multiplication – Shapes

__VOCABULARY:__

__Math:__ sum, difference, product

__Shapes:__ square, circle, pentagon, oval, octagon, rhombus, triangle, rectangle, hexagon, trapezoid

__LANGUAGE STRUCTURE:__

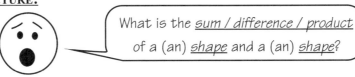

What is the _sum / difference / product_ of a (an) _shape_ and a (an) _shape_?

__DIRECTIONS:__

–Follow the beginning portion of the "addition and subtraction" information gap activity. Set up the web as explained. Input:

Sum means to add.

Difference means to subtract.

Product means to multiply.

–Present the language structures using the word bubbles in the Appendix.

–Choose two shapes from the web and, following the language structures above, ask students to find the sum of the two shapes. Then ask for the difference. Then the product.

–Have student volunteers ask the class for the sum, product, or difference of any two shapes.

__INFORMATION GAP__

Have the students sit in pairs. Prop open a file folder between the students (or any other barrier that still allows for communication). Hand sheets A to one partner and sheets B to the other.

Provide the following instructions:

● On your first sheet, there is a box. The box has shapes with numbers in them. Your partner has shapes with different numbers than the ones in your shapes.

● You must ask your partner for the answers to the problems on your sheet. (Remember to use the language structures)

● Your partner must use the shapes in his box to give you the answers.

● When he gives you an answer, draw a line to that answer on your connect–the–dots page. (Begin where it says "Start.")

● Make sure you ask your questions in order. Connect each answer on the connect–the–dots page to the previous answer.

● Take turns.

● When you are finished, compare your connect–the–dots pages.

*Modification for younger students:

Have younger students first get all seven answers and record them next to the equations on the question page. Then they can be given the connect–the–dots pages and be instructed to connect their answers in the order that they were given.

What is the *sum / difference / product*
of a (an) *shape* and a (an) *shape* ?

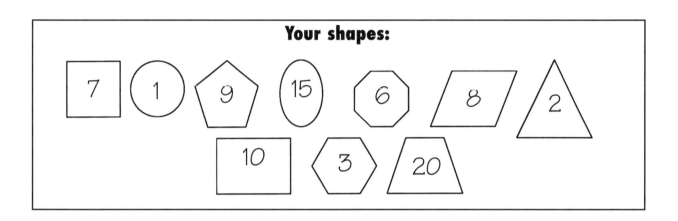

Ask your partner:

1. difference

2. product

3. sum

4. sum

5. difference

6. product

7. product

© 2003 Nicholas V. Flammia

MATHEMATICAL LANGUAGE A

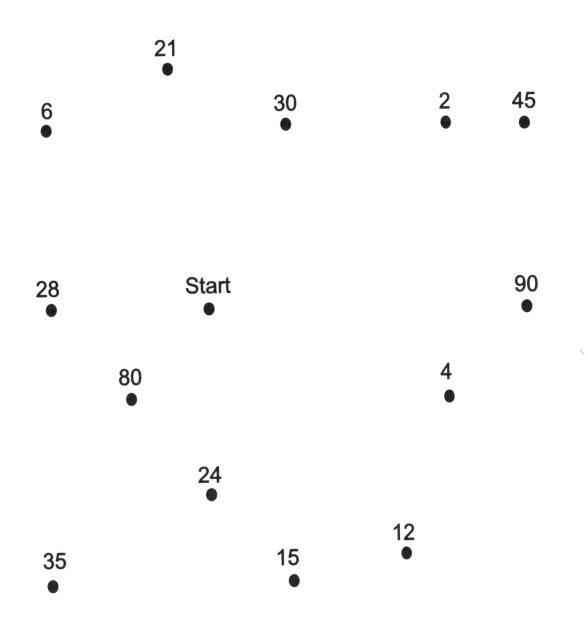

21

6   30   2   45

28   Start   90

80   4

24

12

35   15

© 2003 NICHOLAS V. FLAMMIA

Name:_____ **Mathematical Language – B**

What is the _sum / difference / product_
of a (an) _shape_ and a (an) _shape_ ?

Your shapes:

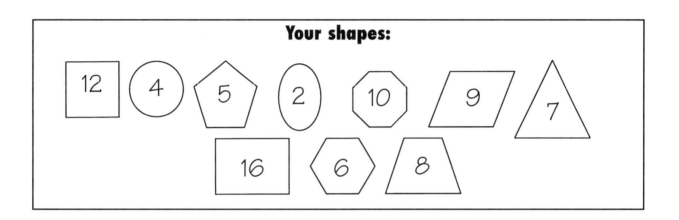

Ask your partner:

1. sum

2. difference

3. product

4. product

5. sum

6. difference

7. sum

© 2003 NICHOLAS V. FLAMMIA

MATHEMATICAL LANGUAGE B

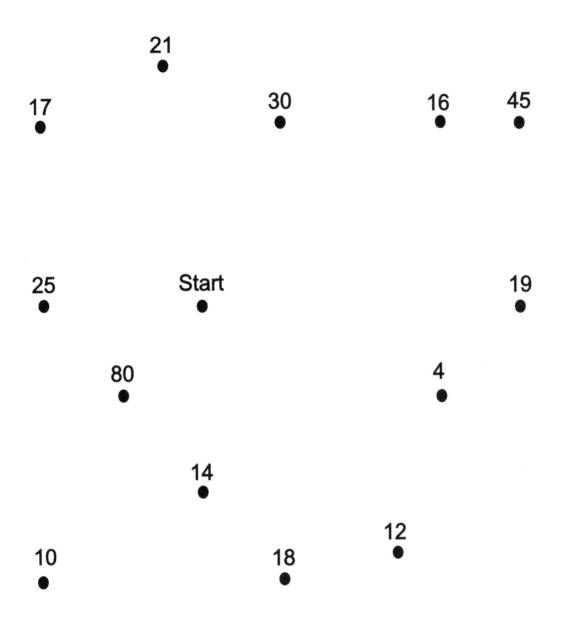

21

17

30

16

45

25

Start

19

80

4

14

12

10

18

© 2003 Nicholas V. Flammia

DIVISION

CONTENT: Math – Division

VOCABULARY:

Math: divisor, dividend, quotient

LANGUAGE STRUCTURE:

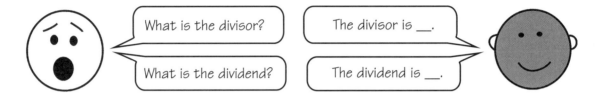

What is the divisor? The divisor is __.

What is the dividend? The dividend is __.

DIRECTIONS:

–Explain that a division equation has 3 parts:

$$\text{divisor} \leftarrow 5\overline{)10} \xrightarrow{\text{2}} \begin{array}{l} \text{quotient} \\ \text{dividend} \end{array}$$

–Explain that in order to solve a division problem, or to get the quotient, we need a divisor and a dividend.

INFORMATION GAP

Have the students sit in pairs. Prop open a file folder between the students (or any other barrier that still allows for communication). Hand sheet A to one partner and sheet B to the other. Each partner should also be given a red, yellow, blue, and orange marker.

Provide the following instructions:

- There are 25 boxes on your sheet. Each box has a number on the top and a division problem on the bottom. Most of the division problems are incomplete.

- You must ask your partner for the missing divisors or dividends. For example: "Box 14: What is the dividend?"

- Your partner must look at his box in order to give you the missing number.

- When he gives you an answer, write it where it belongs.

- Take turns.

- When you are finished, follow the instructions at the bottom of your sheet.

Name:_____ **Division – A**

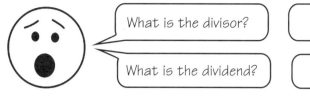
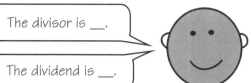

1	2	3	4	5
5⟌25	⟌12	⟌24	9⟌	⟌16
6	**7**	**8**	**9**	**10**
⟌36	⟌45	7⟌14	6⟌48	5⟌30
11	**12**	**13**	**14**	**15**
3⟌9	6⟌	8⟌	4⟌4	6⟌18
16	**17**	**18**	**19**	**20**
⟌36	⟌24	9⟌	7⟌	4⟌16
21	**22**	**23**	**24**	**25**
7⟌56	⟌81	7⟌	⟌24	6⟌

<u>**When you are finished:**</u>

1) Solve

2) Color: **If the quotient is 5 or 8, color the box red.**

   If the quotient is 1 or 2, color the box yellow.

   If the quotient is 3, color the box blue.

   If the quotient is 4, 9, or 6, color the box orange.

3) Compare

© 2003 Nicholas V. Flammia

What is the divisor? The divisor is __.

What is the dividend? The dividend is __.

1	2	3	4	5
)25	3)12	8)	)54	2)16
6	**7**	**8**	**9**	**10**
9)	9)45	)14	)48	5)
11	**12**	**13**	**14**	**15**
3)9	)6	8)16	4)	)18
16	**17**	**18**	**19**	**20**
4)36	3)24	)18	7)35	4)
21	**22**	**23**	**24**	**25**
)56	9)	)21	6)	6)30

When you are finished:

1) Solve

2) Color: If the quotient is 5 or 8, color the box red.

If the quotient is 1 or 2, color the box yellow.

If the quotient is 3, color the box blue.

If the quotient is 4, 9, or 6, color the box orange.

3) Compare

76

© 2003 NICHOLAS V. FLAMMIA

<u>CONTENT:</u>   Math – Fractions

<u>VOCABULARY:</u>
<u>Location:</u> first, middle, last
<u>Fractional Parts:</u> half, third/thirds, fourth/fourths, fifth/fifths, sixth/sixths, seventh/sevenths, eighth/eighths, ninth/ninths
<u>Fractions</u>

<u>LANGUAGE STRUCTURE:</u>

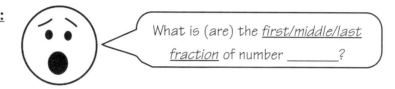

What is (are) the *first/middle/last fraction* of number _____?

<u>DIRECTIONS:</u>
–Write a word and explain that it is a collection of letters (For example, "love" is a collection of four letters: l, o, v, and e).
–Explain that each letter, or part, of the collection has a special name depending on how many letters there are in the collection (For example: The word "love" has four letters, so each letter is called a fourth).
–Ask students for fractional parts of that word, writing the fraction on the board (For example: What is the first 1/4 of "love"? – answer: l. What is the middle 2/4 of "love"? – answer: ov. What is the last 1/4 of "love"? – answer: e.
–Ask the students for words (or names) with 2, 3, 5, 6, 7, 8, and 9 letters and list what the parts are called on the board (halves, thirds, fourths, etc.).
– Give students practice asking and giving fractional parts of these words. Stress that when the numerator is 1, we are only talking about 1 part and therefore leave the 's' off. Example: <u>one</u> third vs. <u>two</u> thirds.

<u>INFORMATION GAP</u>
Have the students sit in pairs. Prop open a file folder between the students (or any other barrier that still allows for communication). Hand sheet A to one partner and sheet B to the other. Place the answer sheet between the students so that it is visible and accessible to both.

Provide the following instructions:
(Model the first number with the class.)

● There is an "ask" column and a "listen" column.

● Partner A looks at his "ask" column and asks his question.

● Partner B looks at his "listen" column and tells partner A the letters that he is asking about.

● Partner A records them on the shared answer sheet next to the number of the question, one letter per box.

● Partner B then looks at his "ask" column and asks his question.

● Partner A looks at his "listen" column and tells partner B the letters that he is asking about.

● Partner B records them next to the previously recorded letters to make a word.

● Go on to the next numbers in the same manner.

● When finished, read the answers on the answer sheet in order.

What is (are) the *first/middle/last fraction* of number _____?

ASK	LISTEN
1 What are the **first** $\frac{2}{4}$?	1 lunch
2 What are the **middle** $\frac{3}{9}$?	2 corn
3 What is the **middle** $\frac{1}{5}$?	3 food
4 What are the **last** $\frac{2}{5}$?	4 wet
5 What are the **first** $\frac{4}{7}$?	5 trumpet
6 What are the **first** $\frac{2}{8}$?	6 pancakes
7 What is the **first** $\frac{1}{2}$?	7 empty
8 What are the **middle** $\frac{2}{4}$?	8 different
9 What are the **first** $\frac{3}{7}$?	9 tenth
10 What is the **last** $\frac{1}{6}$?	10 fast
11 What are the **middle** $\frac{2}{6}$?	11 little
12 What are the **last** $\frac{4}{5}$?	12 bowl

  © 2003 Nicholas V. Flammia

What is (are) the *first/middle/last*
fraction of number _____?

LISTEN		ASK			
1	easy	1	What are the **last**	$\frac{2}{5}$	?
2	chocolate	2	What are the **middle**	$\frac{2}{4}$	?
3	whole	3	What is the **first**	$\frac{1}{4}$	?
4	month	4	What is the **middle**	$\frac{1}{3}$	?
5	special	5	What are the **first**	$\frac{4}{7}$	?
6	macaroni	6	What are the **last**	$\frac{3}{8}$	?
7	up	7	What is the **middle**	$\frac{1}{5}$	?
8	long	8	What is the **middle**	$\frac{1}{9}$	?
9	several	9	What is the **last**	$\frac{4}{5}$	?
10	potato	10	What is the **first**	$\frac{1}{4}$	?
11	mother	11	What is the **last**	$\frac{1}{6}$	?
12	train	12	What are the **first**	$\frac{3}{4}$	?

© 2003 Nicholas V. Flammia

Answer Sheet

1											
2											
3											
4											
5											
6											
7											
8											
9											
10											
11											
12											

© 2003 Nicholas V. Flammia

MONEY – STATIONERY STORE – SUPERMARKET – DEPARTMENT STORE

CONTENT: Math – Money

VOCABULARY:

Math:	dollars, cents
Stationery Store:	stamps, ruler, pen, glue, newspaper, pencil sharpener, greeting card, notebook, eraser, backpack, scissors, pencil, calculator, envelopes, markers, binder
Supermarket:	tea, onion, apple, milk, lemon, chicken, juice, pineapple, steak, bananas, carrots, soda, mushrooms, grapes, watermelon, broccoli
Department Store:	belt, umbrella, scarf, telephone, shirt, candle, tie, t–shirt, picture frame, sweater, sneakers, comb, plates, hammer, socks, skirt

LANGUAGE STRUCTURE:

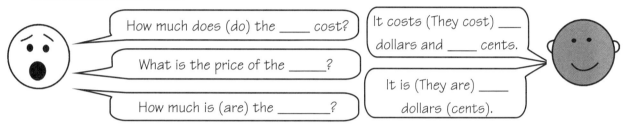

How much does (do) the _____ cost?

What is the price of the _____?

How much is (are) the _____?

It costs (They cost) _____ dollars and _____ cents.

It is (They are) _____ dollars (cents).

DIRECTIONS:

(These directions are for any one of the "Money" information gap activities.)

–Ask students what things they could buy at a stationery store (or supermarket, or department store.) Make a web on the chalkboard with the answers that they suggest. Add any additional items in the vocabulary that they did not mention. Example:

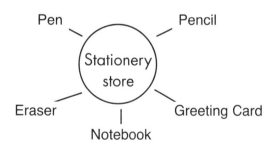

–Ask students how much an item on the web might cost. Write the prices they suggest next to some of the items, making sure to include prices of more than a dollar and less than a dollar.

- Explain how we read money values:

$$\text{dollar(s)} \longrightarrow \overset{\overset{\text{and}}{\vee}}{\$5.10}\text{ cents} \longleftarrow$$

$$10\cent \text{ cents} \longleftarrow$$

–Present the language structures using word bubbles from the Appendix. Model asking and telling the prices of various items. (Stress the use of the appropriate language structure for singular and plural items.)

–Have student volunteers practice asking other students in the class the costs of the items.

INFORMATION GAP

Have the students sit in pairs. Prop open a file folder between the students (or any other barrier that still allows for verbal communication). Hand sheet A to one partner and sheet B to the other.

Provide the following instructions:

- Each of you has a picture of a store shelf. Some of the items don't have prices. You must ask your partner for the missing prices.

- Your partner must look at his store shelf, find the item, and then tell you the price.

- When he tells you the price, write it where it belongs.

- Take turns.

- After you have all your prices, answer the question at the bottom.

- When you are finished, compare your sheets. Do your prices match? Do your totals match?

How much does
(do) the ____ cost?

What is the price
of the _____?

How much is (are)
the _____?

It costs (They cost) ___
dollars and ____ cents.

It is (They are) _____
dollars (cents).

	49¢		$5.49
	86¢	80¢	
		$3.33	6¢
$2.05			$4.62

What is the total cost of all the items? _____

© 2003 Nicholas V. Flammia

Name:_____ **Stationery Store – B**

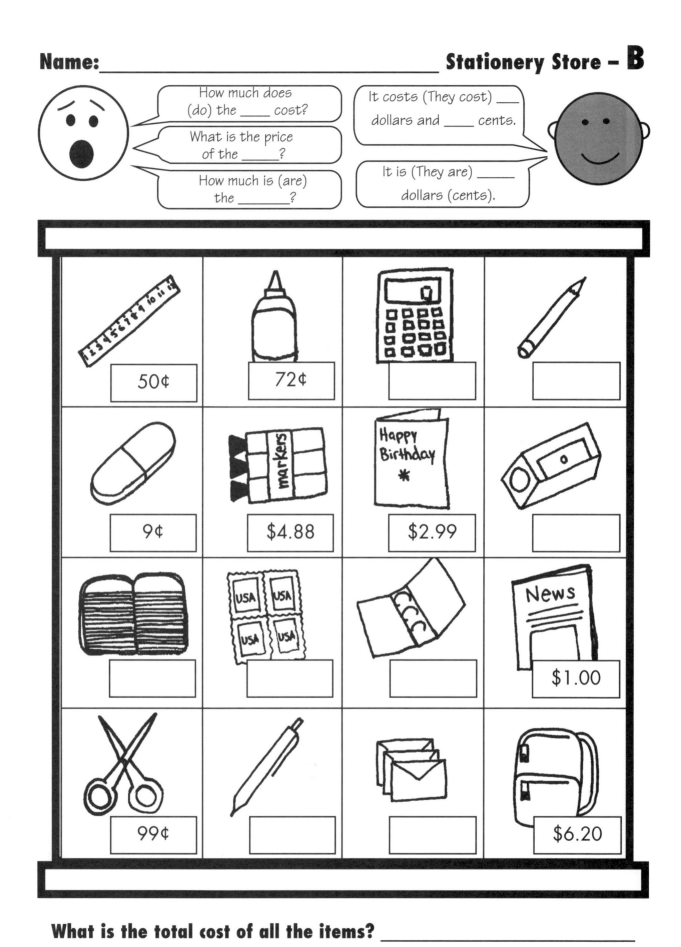

What is the total cost of all the items? _____

                                    © 2003 NICHOLAS V. FLAMMIA

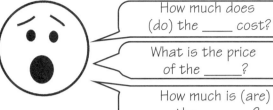

How much does (do) the _____ cost?

What is the price of the _____?

How much is (are) the _____?

It costs (They cost) ___ dollars and ____ cents.

It is (They are) _____ dollars (cents).

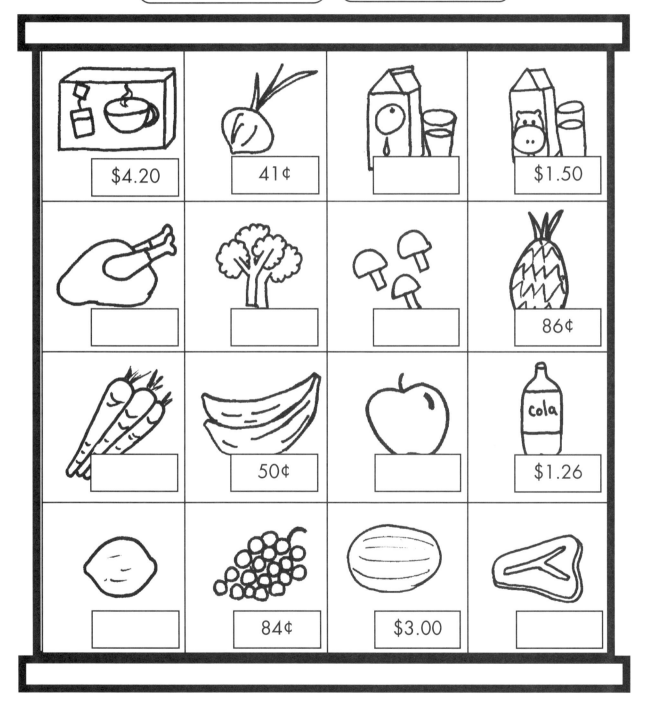

$4.20   41¢ $1.50

         86¢

        50¢ $1.26

        84¢ $3.00

What is the total cost of all the fruits? _____

© 2003 Nicholas V. Flammia

How much does (do) the _____ cost?

What is the price of the _____?

How much is (are) the _____?

It costs (They cost) _____ dollars and _____ cents.

It is (They are) _____ dollars (cents).

32¢

$5.00

$7.99

75¢

$1.99

99¢

85¢

$2.00

What is the total cost of all the fruits? _____

© 2003 NICHOLAS V. FLAMMIA

How much does
(do) the _____ cost?

What is the price
of the _____?

How much is (are)
the _____?

It costs (They cost) ___
dollars and ____ cents.

It is (They are) _____
dollars (cents).

	$10.00		
$14.89	75¢	$7.99	
	$14.99	$9.99	
	$4.25		$9.20

What is the total cost of all the articles of clothing? _____

© 2003 NICHOLAS V. FLAMMIA

How much does (do) the ____ cost?

What is the price of the _____?

How much is (are) the _____?

It costs (They cost) ___ dollars and ____ cents.

It is (They are) _____ dollars (cents).

$12.99		$8.30	99¢
	$3.66	$6.50	
		$5.00	
	$20.00		$11.44

What is the total cost of all the articles of clothing? _____

© 2003 NICHOLAS V. FLAMMIA

CONTENT: Math – Time, Language Arts – Grammar

VOCABULARY:

Time: o'clock, (time expressed in exact hours)
Actions: Focus on third person present tense – (he)
    wake up, make breakfast, start school, eat lunch, walk home, finish homework,
    prepare dinner, watch television, read a book, go to bed

LANGUAGE STRUCTURE:

What does he do at *time*?

When does he *activity*?

He *activity* at *time*?

DIRECTIONS:

–Define "schedule". Introduce a fictional male character. Ask students what activities this character might do every day. Make a web of student responses. Add the verbs in the vocabulary if they have not been mentioned.

–Use the verbs in the web to drill students on the third person present tense. Examples: He eats. He wakes up. He goes to bed.

–Display an analog clock and a digital clock. Explain that these are two ways to show time. Demonstrate how the same time looks on both clocks. (This information gap activity focuses on exact hours, so it would be appropriate to demonstrate times such as 12:00, 1:00, 2:00, etc.)

–Draw the language structures on the chalkboard (or use the word bubbles in the Appendix).

–Choose a verb from the web and model, asking, "When does he (the character) *activity*?" Display one of the previously demonstrated times on the digital or analog clock (exact hour) and model answering, "He *activity* at *time*." Inversely, ask, "What does he do at *time*?"

–Have student volunteers set the clocks and ask the class to respond to a question from the language structures.

INFORMATION GAP

Have the students sit in pairs. Prop open a file folder between the students (or any other barrier that still allows for verbal communication). Hand sheets A to one partner and sheets B to the other.

Provide the following instructions:

● Imagine that this is a schedule for your brother's day. You must finish his schedule by filling in all the analog times, the digital times, and the activities.

● Ask your partner for the times and activities that are missing from your brother's schedule.

● Take turns.

● When you are finished, compare your sheets. Do the schedules match?

WRITING FOLLOW –UP:

–Use the Information Gap Activity Sheet to write a paragraph about an imaginary person. (Morning, afternoon, and evening can be introduced.) Topic Sentence: *My brother has a busy day every Monday.*

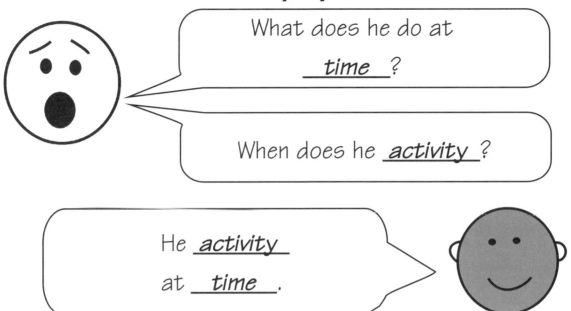

Every Day

What does he do at
__*time*__?

When does he __*activity*__?

He __*activity*__
at __*time*__.

Schedule

Time		Activity
(clock) (digital clock :)		wake up
(clock) (digital clock 7:00)		make breakfast
(clock showing 9:00) (digital clock :)		start school

 © 2003 Nicholas V. Flammia

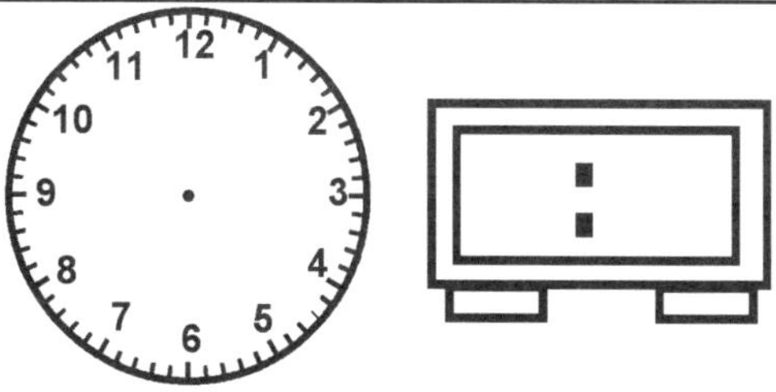	eat lunch
	walk home
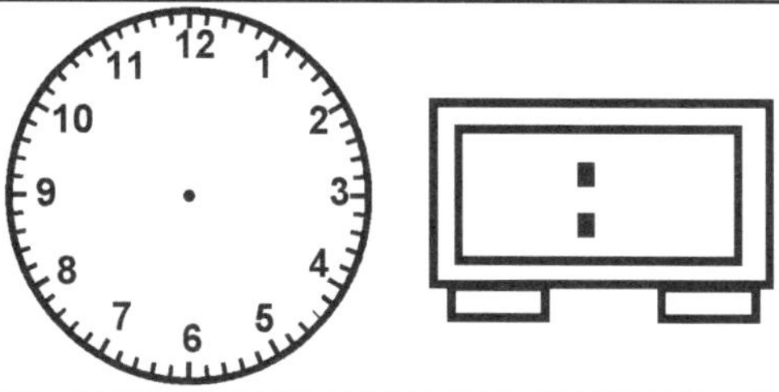	finish homework

	watch television

	go to bed

© 2003 Nicholas V. Flammia

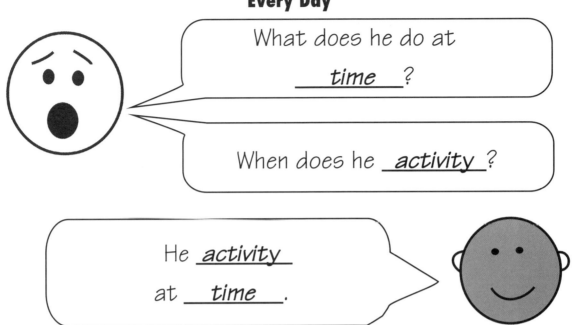

Every Day

What does he do at
___time___?

When does he _activity_?

He _activity_
at ___time___.

Schedule

TIME		ACTIVITY
(clock showing 6:00)	(digital clock :)	wake up
(blank clock)	(digital clock 7:00)	
(blank clock)	(digital clock :)	start school

© 2003 NICHOLAS V. FLAMMIA

(clock showing 12:00)	(digital clock, blank)	**eat lunch**
(clock, blank)	3:00	
(clock showing 3:20)	(digital clock, blank)	**finish homework**
(clock, blank)	6:00	**prepare dinner**
(clock, blank)	(digital clock, blank)	**watch television**
(clock showing 9:00)	(digital clock, blank)	**read a book**
(clock, blank)	11:00	

TIME – YESTERDAY

CONTENT: Math – Time, Language Arts – Grammar

VOCABULARY:
    Time: (time not measured to exact hours)
    Actions: Focus on third person past tense – (she)
        prepare breakfast, drop children off at school, walk to work, start work, finish work, clean the house, fix dinner, visit friends, watch television, use the computer

LANGUAGE STRUCTURE:

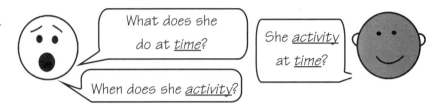

DIRECTIONS:
–This activity is an extension of the previous "Time – Every Day" information gap activity. Similar directions can be followed. However, this information gap activity is designed to focus on **regular past tense verbs**. The times in this activity include times that are **not** on the exact hour.

    Input:
      A. Verbs: The regular past tense is formed by adding 'ed' to verbs or 'd' to verbs that end in 'e'.
      B. Time: Say the hour, and then say the minutes.
        (More advanced forms can be introduced if appropriate. Examples: *minutes* after *hour*, *minutes* to *hour*.)

INFORMATION GAP
Have the students sit in pairs. Prop open a file folder between the students (or any other barrier that still allows for verbal communication). Hand sheets A to one partner and sheets B to the other.

Provide the following instructions:

● Imagine that this schedule shows what your aunt (or any other adult female) did yesterday. You must finish her schedule by filling in all the analog times, the digital times, and the activities.

● Ask your partner for the times and activities that are missing from your aunt's schedule.

● Take turns.

● When you are finished, compare your sheets. Do the schedules match?

WRITING FOLLOW–UP:
–Use the Information Gap Activity Sheet to write a paragraph about the day that the person had. (Morning, afternoon, and evening can be included.) <u>Topic Sentence:</u> *My aunt had a busy day yesterday.*

Name:_____   **A**

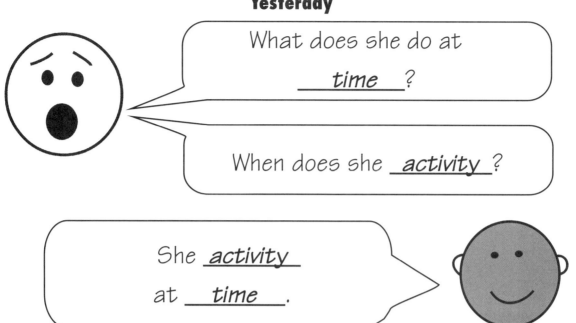

Yesterday

What does she do at ___time___?

When does she ___activity___?

She ___activity___ at ___time___.

Schedule

TIME	ACTIVITY
(analog clock, no hands) : (blank digital clock)	prepare breakfast
(analog clock, no hands) 7:40	drop the children off at school
(analog clock showing 9:10) : (blank digital clock)	

© 2003 Nicholas V. Flammia

(analog clock, no hands)	10:08	**start work**
(analog clock, hands at ~9:18)	:	**finish work**
(analog clock, no hands)	:	**clean the house**
(analog clock, hands at ~6:00)	:	
(analog clock, hands at ~8:20)	:	**visit friends**
(analog clock, no hands)	:	**watch television**
(analog clock, no hands)	10:05	**use the computer**

© 2003 NICHOLAS V. FLAMMIA

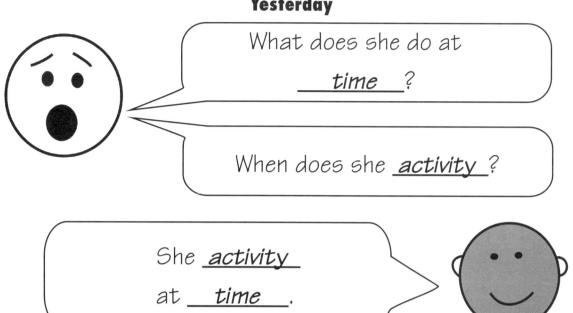

Yesterday

What does she do at
___*time*___?

When does she *activity*?

She *activity*
at ___*time*___.

Schedule

TIME	ACTIVITY
	prepare breakfast
	drop the children off at school
9:10	walk to work

© 2003 Nicholas V. Flammia

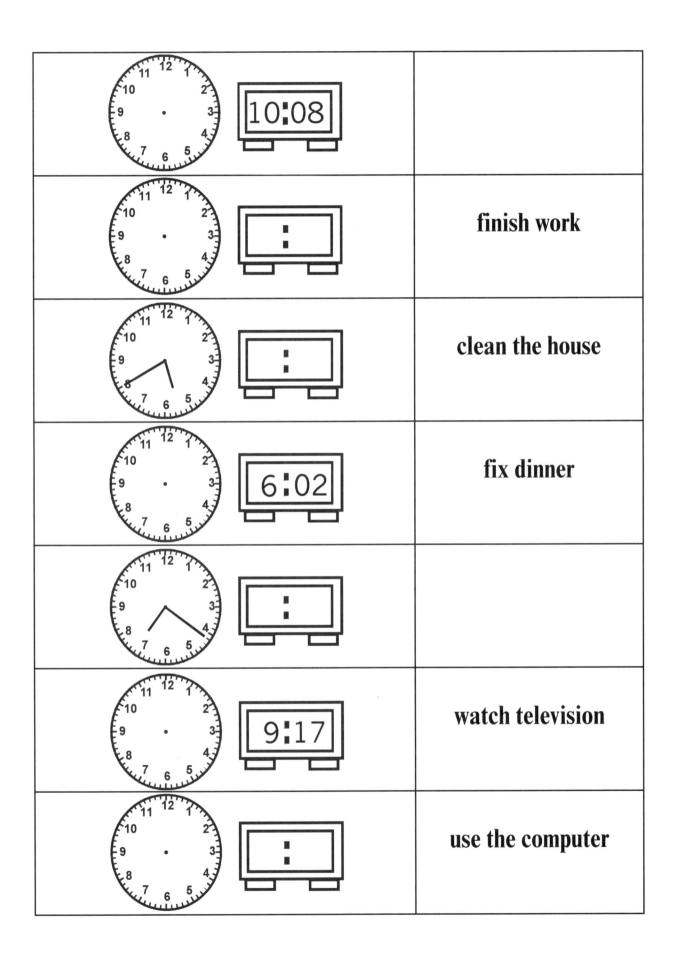

[clock face]	10:08	
[clock face]	[blank digital]	finish work
[clock face ~8:20]	[blank digital]	clean the house
[clock face]	6:02	fix dinner
[clock face ~8:20]	[blank digital]	
[clock face]	9:17	watch television
[clock face]	[blank digital]	use the computer

© 2003 NICHOLAS V. FLAMMIA

TIME – YESTERDAY (IRREGULAR VERBS)

CONTENT: Math – Time, Language Arts – Grammar

VOCABULARY:
Time: *hour* thirty, half past *hour*
Actions: Focus on third person **irregular** past tense – (she)
wake up, eat breakfast, get ready, begin work, drive home, go shopping, eat dinner,
read newspaper, make tomorrow's lunch, go to sleep

LANGUAGE STRUCTURE:

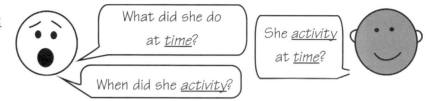

DIRECTIONS:
–This activity is an extension of the previous two information gap activities, "Time – Every Day" and "Time –
Yesterday." Similar directions can be followed. However, this information gap activity is designed to focus on
irregular past tense verbs. The times in this activity include only times that are thirty minutes after the hour.
Input:
A. Verbs: Drill students on the third person irregular past tense verbs in the vocabulary.
B. Time: half past *hour*, *hour* thirty

INFORMATION GAP
Have the students sit in pairs. Prop open a file folder between the students (or any other barrier that still allows
for verbal communication). Hand sheets A to one partner and sheets B to the other.

Provide the following instructions:

● Imagine that this schedule shows what your mother (or any other adult female) did yesterday. You must
finish her schedule by filling in all the analog times, the digital times, and the activities.

● Ask your partner for the times and activities that are missing from your mother's schedule.

● Take turns.

● When you are finished, compare your sheets. Do the schedules match?

WRITING FOLLOW–UP:
– Use the Information Gap Activity sheet to write a paragraph about the day that the person had. (Morning,
afternoon, and evening can be included.) <u>Topic Sentence:</u> *My mother had a busy day yesterday.*

Name:_____ **A**

Yesterday (Irregular Verbs)

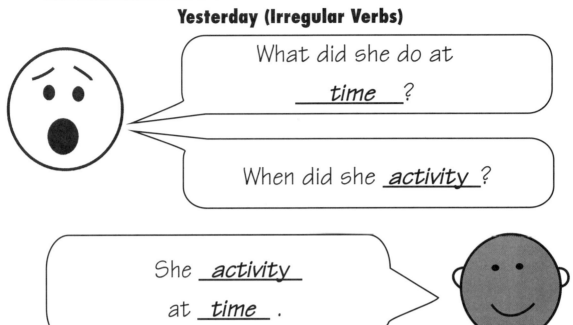

What did she do at
____time___?

When did she _activity_ ?

She _activity_
at _time_ .

Schedule

TIME		ACTIVITY
(clock)	:	wake up
(clock)	7:30	eat breakfast
(clock 9:30)	:	

© 2003 NICHOLAS V. FLAMMIA

	10:30	**begin work**
		drive home
		go shopping
		read the newspaper
		make tomorrow's lunch
	10:30	**go to sleep**

© 2003 NICHOLAS V. FLAMMIA

Name:_____ **B**

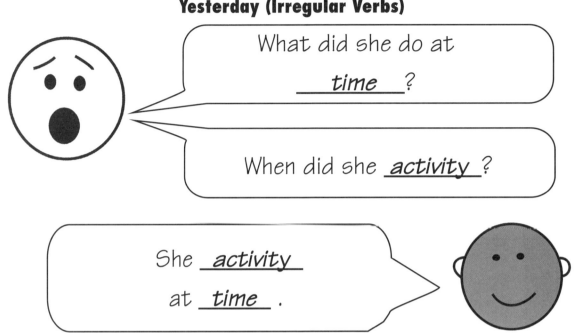

Yesterday (Irregular Verbs)

What did she do at _____?

When did she _activity_ ?

She _activity_ at _time_ .

Schedule

TIME		ACTIVITY
		wake up
		eat breakfast
	9:30	get ready

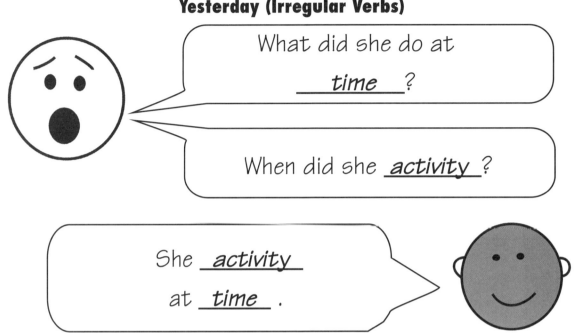

102   © 2003 NICHOLAS V. FLAMMIA

(clock face, no hands)	10:30	
(clock face, no hands)	(blank digital clock)	drive home
(clock face, hands near 6)	(blank digital clock)	go shopping
(clock face, no hands)	6:30	eat dinner
(clock face, hands near 7)	(blank digital clock)	
(clock face, no hands)	9:30	make tomorrow's lunch
(clock face, no hands)	(blank digital clock)	go to sleep

TIME – TOMORROW

CONTENT: Math – Time, Language Arts – Grammar

VOCABULARY:
  Time: a quarter past *hour*, a quarter to *hour*
  Actions: Focus on future tense (they)
  get to school, take the train, arrive in the city, take a tour, visit the museum, eat, see the show, buy souvenirs, take the train home, arrive home

LANGUAGE STRUCTURE:

What will they do at *time*?

When will they *activity*?

They will *activity* at *time*?

DIRECTIONS:

–Begin by telling the students that a class in the school will be going on a trip to the city tomorrow.

–This activity is an extension of the previous three information gap activities, "Time – Every Day," "Time – Yesterday," and "Time – Yesterday (Irregular Verbs)." Similar directions can be followed. However, the times in this activity include only times that are fifteen minutes after the hour and fifteen minutes to the hour. It also focuses on the future tense.

  Input:
   A. Verbs: Add "will" in front of the verb.
   B. Time: a quarter past *hour*, a quarter to *hour*

INFORMATION GAP

Have the students sit in pairs. Prop open a file folder between the students (or any other barrier that still allows for verbal communication). Hand sheets A to one partner and sheets B to the other.

Provide the following instructions:

● Imagine that this schedule shows what the class will do tomorrow. You must finish their schedule by filling in all the analog times, the digital times, and the activities.

● Ask your partner for the times and activities that are missing from the class's schedule.

● Take turns.

● When you are finished, compare your sheets. Do the schedules match?

WRITING FOLLOW–UP:

–Use the Information Gap Activity sheet to write a letter to parents telling them of the trip. (morning, afternoon, and evening can be included.) <u>Topic Sentence:</u> *Your child's class will take a trip to the city tomorrow.*

Name:_____

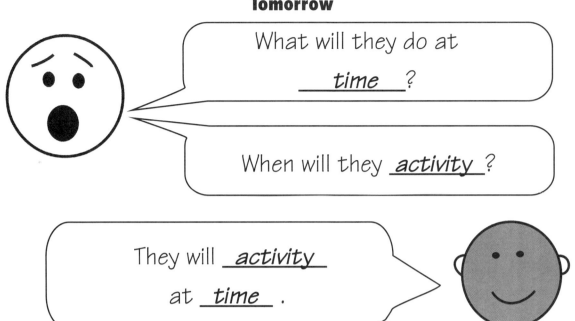

Tomorrow

What will they do at ___*time*___?

When will they _*activity*_?

They will _*activity*_ at _*time*_ .

Schedule

TIME		ACTIVITY
(clock)	⟦ : ⟧	**get to school**
(clock)	⟦ 9:15 ⟧	
(clock)	⟦ : ⟧	**arrive in the city**

© 2003 NICHOLAS V. FLAMMIA

		take a tour
	11:45	**visit the museum**
		eat
	2:15	**see the show**
	5:15	**take the train home**
		arrive home

© 2003 NICHOLAS V. FLAMMIA

Tomorrow

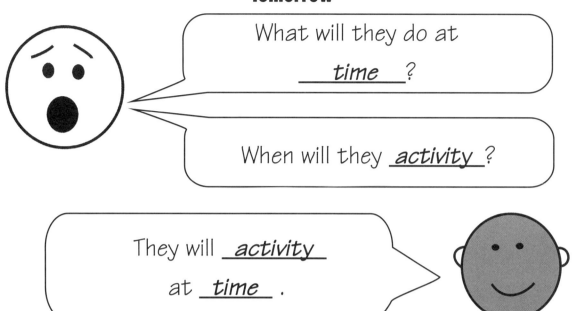

What will they do at
_____time_____?

When will they _activity_?

They will _activity_
at _time_ .

Schedule

TIME		ACTIVITY
(clock) 8:45		get to school
(clock) :		take the train to the city
(clock) 9:45		arrive in the city

		take a tour
		eat
	2:15	
		buy souvenirs
		take the train home
	5:45	**arrive home**

© 2003 NICHOLAS FLAMMIA

The following "listener" and "speaker" pictures and word bubbles can be photocopied and laminated.

When language structures are introduced, they can be written in the word bubbles with dry-erase marker and displayed on a wall, next to the "listener" and "speaker" pictures, for student reference.

Erase the word bubbles and reuse them for each new Information Gap activity!

© 2003 Nicholas V. Flammia

© 2003 Nicholas V. Flammia

111

© 2003 Nicholas V. Flammia

© 2003 Nicholas V. Flammia

113